WHY I STAND

WHY I STAND

JONATHAN ISAAC

Why I Stand

ISBN: 978-1-956007-06-0

Cover design: Ralph Watson
Jacket design: David Fassett
Cover photo: Ashley Landis/Pool/Getty Images

First Edition

Published by DW Books
DW Books is a division of Daily Wire

Daily Wire
1831 12th Avenue South
Suite 460
Nashville, TN 37203
www.dailywire.com

PRINTED IN THE USA

DEDICATION

I dedicate this book to the men and women

who will choose to stand in the days to come.

May the truth always be your aim and

the love of God your guide.

PRAISE FOR *WHY I STAND*

"Jonathan Isaac has it all: brawn, brains, and—most important of all—the humility and moral clarity to use his tremendous gifts for good. Jonathan stands for the flag and kneels only for God at a time when it is not popular to do either. In *Why I Stand*, Jonathan gives us a personal account of how he learned to buck the 'wisdom' of our age and stand tall in the face of pressure. A moving journey."

—MICHAEL KNOWLES

"What a compelling story of God-given courage. I'm so thankful for Jonathan's willingness to consistently stand for truth and to refuse to compromise his values. This book will strengthen your faith in the Lord and equip you to face whatever challenge is before you with boldness and grace."

—ALLIE BETH STUCKEY

"From my experience of spending time with Jonathan Isaac, I have been blessed to watch the Lord move on his heart, in his life and in all he does. He is a great man of God's great love. When I think about the name 'Jonathan' which biblically means, 'God's Gift,' it is perfectly fitting! I believe in my heart that he is a great gift and inspiration for this new generation. We are living in the times where people need to see the demonstration and power of the Holy in our lives. The Gospel has transformed Jonathan's life by the power and outpouring of the Holy Spirit. All people matter to Jesus, and Jonathan knows the price Jesus paid for us all. 'He has the eternal perspective.' He is building God's kingdom, not his own kingdom. He is in the winning business everywhere he goes. 'Winning souls for the Kingdom of God.' I stand with Jonathan Isaac because he is the present and future evangelist doing the great ministry of God, the Great Commission. The supernatural favor of the Lord is on his life, everywhere he goes. Every 'yes' that he has said to Jesus has been the best yeses of his life. It has also given him the greatest reach and eternal impact on millions of souls. We will always be thankful for this. We love him and are very thankful for him. He is a great blessing to us all."

—PASTOR ANWAR FAZAL and NIDA ANWAR FAZAL,
Isaac TV and Eternal Life TV Network

"Nearly seven feet tall isn't what gives Jonathan Judah Isaac courage to stand strong in the face of controversy. It's his deep convictions! While Jonathan has experienced the adulation from crowds as a college and NBA star athlete, he has learned that standing alone is not easy, but it does open doors to sharing our personal faith in Christ. He writes that Jesus is the answer for our problems—from overcoming low self-esteem to championing racial justice. His strong testimony led to Orlando Magic fans nicknaming him 'Minister of Defense.' I like that! As a forward playing on the hardwoods, Jonathan's defensive instincts are admired, but that's not the only thing that sets him apart. Jonathan stood courageously during a time of national conflict, and he has written about his innermost thoughts. Readers will find it compelling to consider just what Jonathan means in his book *Why I Stand*."

—*FRANKLIN GRAHAM*

"I love how authentically Jonathan shares his story. Jonathan's love for Jesus is evident, and his faith is genuine. He shares in his book how God can use anyone, anytime, anywhere and that Jesus is the answer. If you want to be encouraged in how God can use you, pick up a copy of *Why I Stand*."

—*TIM TEBOW*

"When all of his teammates and the rest of the NBA knelt, Jonathan Isaac stood. His story of strength, courage, and sacrifice should inspire anyone facing adversity or being pressured to abandon their values—it should be shared far and wide."

—*BEN SHAPIRO*

CONTENTS

FOREWORD

AS PASTOR AND OVERSEER of JMGC (J.U.M.P. Ministries Global Church), I have been afforded the awesome opportunity to mentor and groom Jonathan Isaac. I have watched this young man soak up every word that is being taught from the pulpit. He's watched my faith-walk and life closely, almost as if he were watching an NBA coach drawing up a play that he would be expected to execute. I've watched him face fear head-on and allow God to change his heart and his life. There is no pretense in the man you meet in this book. This is who he is.

I remember speaking with Jonathan the night before he stood. I told him very clearly, "You cannot stand for God and God not stand for you. Your standing will cause ripples throughout eternity. The impact of this will outlive you, your children, and your children's children." The truth of that is in this book and all that comes because of it.

On July 31, 2020, when Jonathan stood alone on the court, it was not the first time. I've watched Jonathan stand alone throughout the course of his career and personal life. He stood the first time when I asked him to speak at a Sunday morning service, and even more so with asking his teammates to attend. He brought the Word that day as if he had been preaching for years, when in reality, it was his first time ever speaking to a crowd.

When reading this powerful book, you will be inspired by this young man who faced fear and allowed courage to triumph. You will come to understand how courage lies within each of us. You will discover how to experience true victory over the battles we face in our own minds and learn how to speak back to the lying voices and overcome.

It has been said that Steph Curry has changed the face of basketball. We have heard of the NBA greats, Kobe Bryant, Michael Jordan, LeBron James, and Magic Johnson, but ladies and gentlemen, I want to introduce to you the one who has really changed the game. This young man is not just hitting three-pointers and breaking scoring records, he is changing hearts and lives throughout the world. Jonathan Isaac is influencing minds of this generation by demonstrating that love triumphs over fear. I challenge you to read this book and see how a young man's heart was changed from fear and doubt to strength, power, and faith in our Lord Jesus Christ.

This book will not only speak to your mind, it will also speak to your heart. If one's heart is not changed, the mind can never truly be changed. The pages of this book reveal that life in Christ is bigger than basketball.

– Dr. Durone Hepburn (Doc)

INTRODUCTION

EVEN IN THE SAFETY OF THE BUBBLE, I knew full well that what I was about to do would trigger an explosive reaction. The settling dust wouldn't just touch my team, the Orlando Magic, or the NBA; the news of my actions would quickly resound throughout the world.

I didn't make the decision to stand lightly; my experiences have driven my decisions. For many reasons I'll explain, I felt it was the right thing for me to do. Those closest to me lent support, but they weren't in the bubble with me. I stood alone. Sort of. At least that's what all the headlines read—*Jonathan Isaac, "the lone player to stand."* And if your eyes were on me in that moment, you might have thought the same thing. All my teammates wore black T-shirts with the words "Black Lives Matter" spelled out in white letters.

Just before the pre-recorded national anthem played, a swell of rustling bodies thundered inside the protective bubble. Each player, coach, and ref bent downward to the floor, kneeling to symbolize their support for black lives. Some closed their eyes. Some locked arms with neighboring teammates. Others raised their fists in the air. It was meant to be a sign of solidarity.

And during the next two minutes, wearing my white and blue Magic jersey, I stood in the midst of my kneeling teammates, becoming the first player in the NBA not to kneel during the national anthem when the season returned from COVID lockdown hiatus on July 31, 2020.

I didn't fully know what me standing would bring. I knew that harsh criticism of my decision would come almost immediately. I could already hear the frenzied volume of fingers on keyboards, hands on foreheads, and mouths spewing their view of "tolerance." And predictably so, right? I dared to defy someone else's symbolism. I knew some of my teammates would cringe at my stance. I knew others would question my character, my motives. And I knew from that moment on, people would begin to define me based on the stand—without the story.

Despite this, peace surged through me. My breath was stable. My hands did not tremble. My stomach wasn't twisted into a thick knot of paralyzing pressure. I had peace.

The kind of peace I, at one time, never could have imagined was even possible.

You're here because you want to know why I stood. To answer that question, I have to take you on my journey. This is the story behind the stand, the tale of a boy whose life prior to the revelation of Whose he was, was a tangled web of fear, self-doubt, and insecurities.

In this book, you'll see the freedom and peace found in the love of Jesus Christ. My prayer is that you will be inspired with the courage to live beyond the smoke screen of fear and choose to receive and demonstrate the love of God in your everyday life.

I know this because I spent most of my teen and young adult years masking my deeply rooted fears and insecurities behind my basketball ability. My mind was an echo chamber of self-doubt, longing for acceptance and love from my peers. My head full of voices whispering that I wasn't good enough and that no matter how hard I tried, I'd never be.

Through a series of divine connections, being drawn to and pursuing genuine relationships, I finally discovered God's loving intentions toward me. I fought through adversity and showed up, every day, as Jonathan Judah Isaac, fears, flaws, and all, and I progressively got better.

What's your struggle? What are you afraid of? What don't you like about yourself? What are you hiding? What's holding you back? Why won't you stand up? I know where I've been, and I know where I am. More importantly, I know what's made the difference. I want the same thing for you.

I wrote this book to help you find the courage to stand even when you're standing alone. I want the love of God to heal you and the world in the same way it's healing me.

You ready? Let's go!

CHAPTER 1

IT STARTED IN THE BRONX

THE RINGING WAS INCESSANT, as inescapable as a shadow. Unless I powered down my phone, it would continue badgering me with its ringing and vibrating, announcing the name of yet another college basketball head coach who was recruiting me. I remember Rick Pitino from the University of Louisville and John Calipari from the University of Kentucky calling me just minutes apart. And those were just two of the four offer calls I got that night.

This was my life. Great college basketball programs pursued me day and night. They called me. They texted me. They hit up my mom. They sought out my coaches. Relentlessly.

You know when you're going about your day and you remember a scene from a dream you recently had? All of a sudden, you're stuck because you can't remember if it actually happened in real life. Maybe it wasn't a dream?

Yeah, that's pretty much how I felt the entire time I was being recruited for college ball. Was it really happening? Or would I wake up to find it was all a fantasy?

I didn't trust this new reality, and I didn't trust what everyone was selling me. I felt disconnected, like my phone was blowing up for some other Jonathan Judah Isaac, the version of me that could fully embrace this attention. But the real Jonathan—surrounded by accolades I didn't think I deserved, recruited for a level of talent I doubted I had, and promised a golden future that still seemed impossible—floated through the grand experience skeptically.

Unlike many elite athletes, I was not a kid who had visions of playing ball for a fancy college, let alone getting buckets in the NBA. Nah! Not like some of the guys I grew up with. The kids who couldn't stop talking about how life would change once they got to the league or what they would do with all the money. They had the plan, the swag, and more importantly the confidence and sense of identity I viewed as "celebrity." They could sink a clutch jump shot with ease and just keep it moving. League dreams were reserved for their kind.

I was ignorant of the landscape of basketball as a profession. When my phone started ringing with offers, I couldn't tell you the difference between the NCAA (National Collegiate Athletic Association) and the NAACP (National Association for the Advancement of Colored People).

The whole recruiting system was confusing, and after weighing my chances I didn't bother looking it up. I didn't understand what it meant to be a prospect, or what a scholarship offer even looked like. I didn't know a blue-blood program from a community college.

I remember being on the phone with one college coach, and he told me his school was in the best conference. I stammered, "Oh, what's a conference?" For real. That's what I said. Don't judge. At the time I was the number one high school player in my state of Florida, and I had no clue about what came next.

Only two years earlier, when it came to college recruiting, I'd heard crickets. I was a relative no-name, ranked somewhere in the 400s in the nation. Now I was smothered by pitches and promises, golden tickets, and visions of fame. I grew to like it, so no complaints. Remember, I was the kid who never thought any of this was possible. At least for me.

I finally made a plan to end the nonstop ringing. I called the one coach I knew I'd say yes to. The one who believed in me when I was a lanky junior in high school with a big fro and pants that swallowed my rail thin frame and fell half a foot above my ankles.

At the time I made that call, I still didn't know who he or anyone else saw. Every time I looked in the mirror, I was the same skinny kid from the Bronx. Maybe just a little taller.

ROOTS

I grew up in Hunts Point, a neighborhood that runs along the East River in the South Bronx, one of the five boroughs of New York City. The tiny peninsula is dominated by industrial warehouses, repair shops, and apartment buildings with iron-covered windows. My neighborhood, one of the poorest in the country with almost half of its residents living in poverty,[1] was featured in an HBO documentary. *Hookers at the Point* was released in the mid-1990s, a year or two before I was born on October 3, 1997.

Word on the street was that Hunts Point was New York City's red-light district. The documentary profiled the underworld of local prostitutes, showing their far-from-glamorous lifestyle. I never watched the film. And I never saw a sex worker. Or perhaps I wouldn't have known if I did. I guess they came out at night.

My older brother Jacob would see them sometimes. Or maybe he was just old enough to understand things I didn't. He saw a lot more things than I did. He told me one time he went over to our neighbor's house when he was around nine, me seven, and instead of playing video games, he had a real gun shoved into his hands. "You become a real man once you hold one of these," the teen said. My brother remembers the piece being warm and him wanting to run for his life.

We lived in a brick and shingled two-family home on Barretto Street. Our home was sandwiched between another house and a repair shop. My parents rented out the bottom half, but to the best of my knowledge, whatever tenants lived there rarely paid rent, and my parents didn't press them for it.

Pops was a manager at McDonald's in Times Square. The face of that fast food joint fit right into the frenetic backdrop of flashing neon lights and massive digital billboards. There were no golden arches. No red and yellow plastic either. Just the word "McDonald's" lit up by thousands of marquee light bulbs. The three-story, 17,000-square-foot flagship restaurant become a hotel of sorts, but I'll get to that in a minute.

Pops was tall and lean, fit. When I was younger, he was literally Superman in my eyes, especially when he'd pump out a million pushups with me laying on his back. I thought his muscles were so big. Pops was my idol. I looked up to him for everything. Whenever I'd see him come from work or somewhere else, first thing I did was run and jump into his arms, then he'd swing me high, light as a feather, and hug me close. I felt that I was special to him.

Ma worked as a nurse. She was the sweetest momma bear alive. Always cared about others, and never played about her kids. There's no number of jobs too many if it meant giving us a better future.

They both worked a lot and at ungodly hours; their marriage felt like trains passing in different directions.

Many bedtimes for us kids didn't begin with a bath and a story, but with blankets sprawled out in the roped off section on the second floor of the McDonald's where Pops worked the night shift. When they were both working overnight hours, it was easier for us kids to stay with Pops. He would take us straight to school when his shift was over. All four of us—my older sister, Kalilah, my older brothers Jacob and Joel, and I—looked forward to sleepovers at Mickey D's. We'd make forts out of blankets, spy on the late-night customers from our second floor perch, and eventually fall asleep with the smell of Quarter Pounders and Big Macs wafting over our French-fry-stuffed bellies and freshly brushed teeth.

I loved it. What kid wouldn't want to sleep in a Mickey D's? It was almost as good as the bacon, egg, and cheese sandwiches Pops would sometime get us from the corner deli before dropping us off at school. My favorite side was these mini candy hamburgers selling for a nickel. For just a buck, I could stuff my pockets with twenty individually wrapped gummy treats, always biting off the candy bun before sinking my teeth into the squishy and fruit-flavored lettuce, cheese, and meat layer. I liked life simple, and candy squishy.

A REVIVAL REVOLUTIONARY

For our family, church was sacred. Ma and Pops were both God-fearing people, but Pops was the one who forced us to memorize scripture. A lot of it and all the time. As if we didn't get enough at Canaan Land Church, where we spent Sunday mornings, Sunday evenings, Wednesday evenings and the occasional pop-up service on Tuesday nights.

Canaan Land was a Pentecostal church, which may mean nothing to you, but if you were born and raised in a Pentecostal church, particularly a black Pentecostal church, you're probably smiling because you get it. Known for their revivalist fervor, churches like ours expressed this passion with loud singing. Robust praying. Fast-paced, pulse-pounding music with jingling tambourines. Services that lasted for hours. A preacher who whooped, using his voice like an instrument, combining art and oratory and passion to a crowd who'd holler "Amen" and rush to their feet with thundering applause after pretty much anything he said. If you didn't get the feels for something in church, you probably didn't have a pulse.

Where did these Pentecostal feels come from? The church's past is a story about the power of unity over division. A story worth telling and, to me, ironically necessary to hear today. In 1870, William Seymour, the son of freed African American slaves, was born in Centerville, Louisiana. Seymour would become one of the founders of the modern-day Pentecostal movement. Seymour spent his younger years in the South where prejudice and poverty permeated every aspect of the culture. In an era when segregation was common in houses of worship, Seymour held a more progressive view. He believed that everyone should be able to worship together. And that meant *everyone*, regardless of what you looked like or where you came from.

When Seymour traveled North to different churches and Bible schools, he was introduced to the theology of the baptism of the Holy Spirit which forever changed him. In Los Angeles, he started hosting a small prayer meeting and Bible study at a friend's home which grew quickly. When the front porch collapsed from the weight of all the people in attendance, Seymour began to look for a church—and he found one, a building that formerly housed a livery stable on Azusa Street in 1906. The first service ignited what became known as the Azusa Street Revival and lasted about three years.

People came in droves. All kinds of people. Men and women. Blacks, whites, Asians, immigrants, rich, poor, illiterate, and educated. You have to remember this was 1906, the height of the Jim Crow era, when segregation laws divided the nation. But if you sat in Pastor Seymour's church, the mushrooming racial tension wasn't evident. A crusader for unity, Seymour "stood at the forefront of one of the most revolutionary social movements in history, a movement, intent upon erasing the color line. This was a movement that did not just seek prophecy but sought to prophetically embody the in-breaking kingdom of God."[2]

Pastor Seymour may have been born in a different century, but he had the right idea. Sadly, division is a familiar face. In the midst of the revival, trouble and division snaked its way in. Bickering broke out among the church leaders about theological differences, the name of the church, and which particular denomination it belonged to. While these irreconcilable differences fractured the miraculous unity a few years after it began, Seymour's efforts exploded the Pentecostal movement around the world, and thousands and thousands of lives were never the same.

LESSONS IN LYING

Although Seymour's Pentecostal tradition is known for high-intensity services, it wasn't rare for me to fall asleep at church. With no kids' programs available, us Isaac children had to sit in the service with our parents. At some point in every service, I'd inevitably feel the spirit of tired fill my soul, and my head would slowly inch back, one exhale at a time, until my chin pointed straight toward the church ceiling and my head would hit the back of the hard wooden pew I sat on. If that thud on my scalp didn't wake up my bored self, a smack on the head from Pops did. I knew God was important because of the way Pops talked about Him, but being so young, I didn't really grasp His utility. Definitely not the spiritual stuff. I didn't know why people would cry out loud when they prayed or worship with their hands raised or get so moved in the Spirit that they'd let loose with some crazy dances that may not have embarrassed them but made me want to giggle or look away.

The Isaac kids were taught to do the right things. Don't cheat. Don't steal. Treat others with kindness and respect. Honor your parents and don't lie. I excelled in most of those things most of the time. I was never much of a troublemaker, but I wasn't a saint either.

I'll never forget when I broke that one commandment about lying. I got a whooping for it. And it wasn't the kind of vocal whooping our preacher did to add 25 minutes to his sermon. We were at church and getting ready to leave. I was eight. I'd just finished gulping down a cup of water and had thrown the paper cup, not in a trash bin, but on the ground under the car. Just before Pops ducked into the driver's seat to drive us home, he noticed the paper object.

"Whose cup is that?"

I froze. "Not mine," I boldly declared. He'd never have known it was me if I hadn't rushed to my own defense.

He gave me a look. You know, the omniscient parental kind. "Jonathan," he said again, this time slowly stretching out my namesake's three syllables. "Whose cup is that?"

"I don't know, Pops," I insisted.

"So where's your cup?"

"I threw mine away inside." My heart rate started a steep climb as the words tumbled out of my mouth. I immediately regretted what I'd just said.

"Show me."

He followed me back inside the church as I did my best to steady my breathing. I didn't even know which garbage can to lead him to that would contain my non-existent used paper cup. I pointed to the one that seemed to attract the most traffic. As I prayed silently in my head on repeat, *Please let there be cups in there,* I watched him bend his lanky frame over the canister. Standing on my tiptoes, from the corner of my eyes I peeked over the metal rim.

Relief swept over me. Saved by the cups! There wasn't just one, but a bunch of them scattered over plates of leftover rice and beans and used napkins.

"See? There's cups right there," I retorted, smugly satisfied with myself.

Before he and Ma tucked us kids into bed that night, Pops indulged us in an impromptu Bible study. I can't remember the scripture or the illustration he used, but the topic was on lying. I know, could Pops be more obvious? Or gracious, giving me an opportunity to confess and make things right. I didn't connect the dots. I just got ready to go to bed and was lights out. No more, no less. It wasn't until the next night after goodnight kisses had been blown, and my brothers and I were tucked tight into our bunk beds, that I rolled over to my side and—

"Mister Jonathan!"

I sat up so fast, the room spun. I knew this was bad. Whenever my dad inserted a "mister" before the name of my brothers and me, it spelled trouble. Specifically, a whooping awaited us. I leapt out of bed and ran to my parents' bedroom. "Yes, sir?" I panted. Fear stung every inch of my body, knowing what was coming. But, for the life of me, I couldn't think for what.

Pops looked me dead in the eyes and spoke with a gentle calm. "So tell me, Mister Jonathan, was that your cup under the car?"

I spoke quietly but with confidence. "No, sir."

Enter the good old-fashioned butt whooping. It wasn't malicious nor was it meant to break my spirit, but it hurt. Not enough to make me come clean though.

A few wallops with a belt on my pajamaed behind and he asked me again. "Jonathan, was that your cup?"

"No," I repeated with so much conviction I think I just about started to believe my own lie.

"Jonathan, it's not good to lie."

"I'm not lying. The cup wasn't mine!" I pleaded.

The cycle of trying to whoop the truth out of me and my stubborn denial lasted for an hour. Or at least that's how long it seemed to me at the time. Looking back, it was probably nowhere near that long. At one point I even told Pops it was Joel's cup! I was all in! He actually woke Joel up only for my brother to deny the obvious. Eventually, I gave up the truth.

So why did I hang onto the unnecessary lie over a silly cup for so long? I truly thought I could make him believe me, and then he'd feel bad. Dumb reasoning, I know. Lesson learned. I think about this silly story every now and then as a reminder of the unforeseeable destruction that lurks behind dishonesty. If Pops had believed me, ultimately feeling bad and letting me off the hook, I would have won the battle but lost the war, eroding the innocence Pops was trying to protect. My father was big into having integrity. If we didn't have that, we had nothing.

LIFE GETS COMPLICATED

Getting whooped was common in our household. Just like shooting hoops was. My dad, my brothers, the neighborhood kids, and I would head to the park courts, rain or shine, to hoop. Not really in a serious way but just for fun. We didn't need anything but ourselves and a ball.

Even at a young age, I defined basketball as art, poetry in motion if you will. The ball bouncing like the beat of a drum. Powerfully graceful movements left to right, right to left, one after another like windshield wipers. All originated in the mind of the baller. It's his or her show. Whenever I'd play ball with the fam, in my mind I'd float. Without the confine of technique or regulation, shooting hoops was a freedom of sorts. I could just be in my own world. As I got older and started playing organized ball, the game became my peace. It morphed into a purpose, my wellbeing. I truly loved it in the simplest sense. It wasn't about being a big-time NBA player, just the ball and the hoop. The game. To this day when it's just me, the lines, the leather, the net, everything else fades to a fuzz.

But life in the Bronx was more complex than Pentecostal church services, hamburger gummies, and shooting hoops. Moms walked home from work one night and heard gunshots. She got spooked. It was also the straw that broke the camel's back on my parents' silently struggling relationship. She was determined to get us kids out of the Bronx. But not with my father.

If there was tension between the two of them, I, ten years old at the time, wasn't fully aware of it. I didn't see dirty fights or hear nasty name-calling. Just occasional frustration boiling over, garden-variety stuff. By the end, they were two separate people just trying to make it work. Vaguely connected by progeny and household responsibility. There was no togetherness, really, no harmony like it used to be.

I have this one sweet memory of them. Pops playfully chasing Moms around the house. We all got in on it, despite being grossed out by their affection. Thinking of it still makes me smile. But by the time Moms was ready to leave, affection was long gone. Pops did his thing, which was church and work. And Ma did hers, work and mother stuff. Pops was more than a few years older than Ma, and he definitely had what I understand today to be a more traditional conservative Christian outlook on marriage and family. Ma, on the other hand, wasn't all the way there.

She was young and outgoing and, most of all, stubborn. She wanted to do things her way. You see the conflict? My marriage counselor diagnosis is: She probably felt voiceless and stifled at times. And Pops? Likely, disrespected and not needed. I adore both of my parents, and I still don't entirely know what ended their relationship. It was their marriage, after all, not mine. What I do know is that after those gunshots rang out, Ma decided it was time to go. Without Pops.

Even all these years later, it's hard for me to write about this time in my childhood. My memory is hazy. If I close my eyes, I can see blurry snapshots of scenes muddled together in a disjointed collection. I remember lots of tears. Hot ones. I'm sure my siblings shed tears, too. I was confused, torn between what felt important at the time but also was clearly out of my control.

Our departure seemed hasty. Barked orders echoed in my ears. Five pairs of hands in bedrooms tossing clothes and toys and books into worn suitcases. Me tailing my older siblings, whimpering like a lost puppy. Everyone was talking all at once, but no one seemed to be saying anything. Someone mentioned Florida, as in the place where we were moving to. *What the heck is Florida?* I remember thinking. It may have been the first time I had even heard of the word. *Is it hot? Is it cold? What's school like? How are the people? And lastly, are there cheese fries? Like the ones at the Kentucky Fried Chicken down on*

Longwood. My favorite! Maybe we could make a pitstop and grab some cheese fries on the way to Florida as a farewell. That'd make me feel better.

Time sped by in a blur. And then, we were gone. No one told me why Pops wasn't with us. One of my older siblings was plopped in the front seat of the car while Moms drove. This arrangement didn't feel right, but it was our new normal. I sat in the back, squashed between legs and luggage in a car that rumbled with tears and moans and questions. There was no preparation for how the restructuring would manifest in my life. I didn't know it then, but I'd never sleep in a McDonald's again or see its name in those big lights ever again. I felt homesick the minute we crossed the George Washington Bridge. I could've told you right then and there that Florida didn't have the kind of cheese fries the Bronx did.

I was right.

CHAPTER 2

CULTURE SHOCK

NEWTON'S FIRST LAW OF MOTION SAYS, "Everything continues in a state of rest unless it is compelled to change by forces impressed upon it." Sir Isaac Newton may have been referring to the laws of physics, but his theory feels like an apt description of the changes that came with my family's move. Nothing was at rest from that point on.

I peppered my siblings with questions. *Where's Pops? Why isn't he with us? Are we going back to New York? Are we going to stay in Florida forever?* They probably knew as much about the situation as I did. We were all in the same boat, rowing for our lives but not knowing where we were going.

Kalilah, the only girl and oldest child, took on a motherly role almost immediately, cooking and cleaning, while Ma was working what seemed like two or even three jobs to put food on the table and pay the bills. Jacob, well, he was always just too cool for school. I think he came out of the womb that way. Definitely too cool for younger brothers and too cool to put much effort into really anything. Secretly, I wished I was more like him. All the girls liked him and for good reason. Confident, good-looking, smooth-talking, a beast on the court. He could command a room with his charm, and he knew it. Jacob never let an opportunity pass to beat me at something. Typical big bro behavior. Joel, who fell into place right after Jacob and before me, was preoccupied with music. Gifted is an understatement. From the time we were really little, instruments were like second fingers to Joel. Winston, the second-to-last child, was a fiery, happy ball of nonstop energy. Did everything with a smile and a dance move. Lastly, and I'm not gonna lie, my favorite, was little bro Jeremiah, whom Ma had a couple months into us being in Florida. And me? I just went along for the ride. Assimilating to the stifling heat and slower pace of life in the Sunshine State was pretty easy after a few days. Unlike processing my dad's absence. I adored my Pops. And certainly things weren't the same without him. But for some reason I didn't think about it much. Like ever. We'd talk from time to time on the phone, but as far as emotions or thoughts of missing him or my old life in New York or why things were the way they were, nothing. Maybe the pain of not seeing him dug a bit deeper than I was comfortable addressing. Maybe ignoring the absence made for better sleep. I'm not sure.

Mom compensated by trying her best to be both parental figures. Something I understand today to be as respectable as it is difficult. She did a great job, providing, nurturing, and trying to juggle everything you get with two parents in one, a feat I'll forever deeply respect and honor. But even as I tried not to think about it, the evidence that the abrupt absence of my superhero played a major role in my development (or lack thereof) soon became crystal clear.

NEW PLACE, NEW TROUBLE

Hunts Points, NY, was a predominantly Hispanic community, rounded out with blacks and a white minority. In Naples, the tables reversed drastically. Now we Isaac kids were the ones that stuck out. Our new hometown boasted one of the highest per capita incomes in the country along with one of the highest proportion of millionaires. Naples was rich rich. Of course, you wouldn't know it from some of the places we lived, bopping around town every few months. I can remember a time or two getting dressed for school by candlelight. Over the years we also had some great spots that made me wonder how in the world we could afford them. Ma worked her butt off. Two, three nursing jobs at a time. But sometimes it wasn't enough.

Insecurities about being accepted in a new environment filled my mind. I feared making a bad first impression. So I did what any kid would do. I tried to fit in. But Naples kids acted a lot different than New York ones.

I was used to the aggressive nature of our horseplay back home. We were rough around the edges. We'd jump on and throw each other around, until we were gassed or reprimanded by a shout of "knock it off." A bruise or two from school was common. It was called socialization.

So when I got to Naples in my last year of elementary school—with the Bronx being very much in my blood—I would stealthily grab kids by the ankles and drag them a couple yards. In the name of social acclimation. No harm, no foul. Onlookers would laugh and even try the same on me. It was my way of getting kids to like me, to show that I was fun and not a threat.

I thought it was working. But one morning, as I initiated my usual rough housing, nobody laughed. To my surprise, these little booger eaters had set me up. The security guard was on standby, and with a swift grab of my shirt, I landed in the principal's office.

"He's just a kid," Ma pleaded with the principal. Sweat dripped from my temples as if the air conditioner wasn't blasting directly on me. I sunk further down into the metal chair feeling smaller than all the kids I was bigger than.

"We cannot tolerate other children being in danger, Mrs. Isaac," the principal spoke, with a concerned tone.

"We've just moved from New York, the Bronx," Ma added. "He's just trying to fit in. Sir, I promise you it won't happen again."

I had been to the principal's office back in New York. I

got scolded by him and whoopings from Pops for making stupid outbursts in class and when roughhousing went too far. But my old principal had always handled me as a case of youthful ignorance. Now I was an alleged danger to the kids around me.

I remember the feeling of shame and embarrassment that washed over me in the principal's office that day. It wasn't because my mom was called or that I got caught or even that someone had set me up. It was that I was so wrong in my perception of myself. In the eyes of my peers, I was exactly what I dreaded being: different. And in my head that day in the principal's office, a monologue took root that would replay in my mind for years.

"They just don't like you."

"What did you expect would happen?"

"You're not cool!"

That negative self-diatribe looped in my head the entire way home. All I cared about was how those kids viewed me and what that implied about who I was. In my mind they were the same.

THE CLASS CLOWN

"Apologize to your classmates, Jonathan, or you're off to the principal's office," my sixth-grade teacher said, exhausted by my daily class clown foolery.

I sat as still as the D.A.R.E. poster plastered on the wall as all eyes were on me.

"Let's go, Jonathan. Just say it."

Two words needed to roll off my tongue. Three syllables, just three, to end the drama. And let's be real, I didn't even have to mean it. Nobody who is forced to say "I'm sorry" is required to be sincere.

What had I done that I needed to apologize for? Oh, just the classic raised-my-hand-and-gave-an-answer-that-made-absolutely-no-sense-at-all. I was in middle school now and determined to be liked. What's more likable than the class clown? To me, apologizing would negate all the laughter I had caused leading up to the teacher's demand for an apology. The kids would think the teacher won, or worse, that I was weak.

The question, *why couldn't I just apologize,* would often cross my mind as I sat in ISS (in school suspension). I was feeling so many different things on the inside from being defective, weak, different, unlikeable, unable to fit in, awkward, too tall, too skinny, too Black. To bend the knee in any way ever, in my mind, would be to affirm them.

Being embarrassed had already become without a doubt my worst fear. It was like the revelation to whoever was around me that I was inadequate. Or so I thought. My prideful knee-jerk reaction, like walking out of class, was to display some type of power move to show I wasn't defeated.

Sixth grade ended on a violent note with two incidents. To me, they weren't who I was, they were the only hands

I had. The first took place in gym class. A kid blasted me with a red rubber ball moments after our teacher already called the dodge ball game. The ball sailed through the air like a missile and landed with a thud on the back of my head. My body convulsed forward to the ground, but my long arms outstretched on the grass saved me from tumbling on my face. I stayed there for a few seconds, hearing the giggles of those watching. I saw red. I leapt off my knees and hightailed it so fast toward him, he didn't have time to escape. Only thing I remember is crushing his neck in a headlock and two teachers trying to pry me off of his body. I may have been scrawny, but in that moment, I wanted to kill him.

Second, and thankfully last, one goes like this. There weren't a ton of black kids at our school, but one guy liked to rap at lunchtime. He thought he was the next Soulja Boy. Hearing him from across the lunchroom, I muttered to the friends I was with that I didn't think he was all that.

"Heard what you're saying, bro," Soulja said, wide-eyed.

"I didn't say anything, bro," I mumbled and quickly gulped down some milk. *This isn't going to end well.*

Soulja decided to mush me in the face! I groaned on the inside. Deep exhale. *I have to retaliate.* If we were alone, I would have just gone in the other direction. But everyone was watching. I shot up from the table and pushed him with everything my skinny frame had. Fists began to fly. I got one good connection in, and the fight was over.

A few minutes later in his office, the principal asked us, "Okay, you two, is this over? Are you guys done?"

Soulja looked down and shrugged. "Yeah, I'm done."

I shook my head. "I'm not done." I mean, between you and me, obviously I was done. I may have been from the Bronx, but fighting really wasn't me. I just didn't want to concede even if he conceded first.

The principal sighed and told Soulja, "Go on, get to class."

The principal gave me another shot, calling my bluff. "Jonathan, I'm going to ask you again," he said. "Are you done?" Long pause as I contemplated my response . . .

"No."

My parting gift was a two-day suspension.

You think maybe I missed my dad?

BIBLES AND BASKETBALL

Only two things really held my attention while I was trying to navigate my Florida existence. Church and basketball.

Church in Naples was the polar opposite of Canaan Land church in optics and delivery. For starters, much less whooping. Friendlier to a degree. And more relaxed. Ma insisted that we go to church from the very beginning of our new life in the Sunshine State. She never had to even say the word "church" when dad was around. It was important to her that we kept the tradition. We quickly got involved in everything.

Jacob was the church drummer, as he was back in the Bronx. Joel, Winston, and Kalilah were part of the worship team (rightfully so, Lord knows the church needed some soul). I pretty much just lurked in the background for a while until I got comfortable with the youth group kids. I eventually found my niche in our youth group skits. We'd act along to a moving song. After a while, I always had a lead role—probably because I wanted to be perfect , so I'd take the skits ten times more seriously than anyone else, but also because I liked the attention that typically followed performances.

Youth group became quite fun, and learning about Jesus wasn't too bad either. The deconstruction from the lofty spiritual place in New York to the more basic level teaching of Christ in Florida made faith easier to digest. I remember at one service awkwardly raising my hand after the leader asked, "Who wants to become a Christian?" A simple prayer and that was that. Overall, youth group helped me breathe. It was a safe place where anxiety would fade and my mind could slow. Still, outside of youth group and inside of me, there was unrest.

Me and my big bro Jacob started playing basketball at the YMCA to pass time after school as I was finishing sixth grade. It was good making friends, but I didn't enjoy playing. I was scrawny, clumsy, and emotionally unstable. Not a player you'd build on 2k. My typical afternoon was spent holding back tears from defeat and Jacob rubbing it in.

To my surprise, when summer began, a buddy asked me if I wanted to play with his travel team. My only appealing feature was my height. And just like that, I became a center for the Naples Phenoms. Long story short, I rode the bench until my last game. I wasn't aggressive like the other kids or really even capable. Then one game the starting center fouled out AND so did his back up. Only one left was yours truly. We were up in a close game with maybe two minutes left. I lost the game for us in a way I refuse to repeat, and the car that usually brought me to practice never showed up again. Yeah, that's how they kicked you off the team back then—without actually telling you.

Later that summer my cousin Dimitri, who had already lived in Florida, mentioned the Estero Airforce. *Great*, I thought, *another travel team*. But this team was different. Coach Bora, the assistant coach at the time, came to our house. After shooting around on our hoop, he asked me to play. He saw something in me I didn't see in myself. So as raw as I was, I made the team, a 5'9 wing learning the ropes. Good thing, too, because he and the head coach, Coach Mark, preached development.

I had a lot of work to do. I needed to work on skill but also learn the actual game too. Like you can't throw the ball back behind the half court line once you've crossed it. My bad. I progressed under Coaches Mark and Bora. Our team was just under . . . bad. Not terrible, but yeah. I remember more defeats than wins. Which didn't do much for my self-confidence. I left a ton of games in tears as I branded myself a failure at life.

Ma would always act a spectacle at the games. I hated it. I was still very much awkward and not in complete control of my body. She would shriek from the stands, "Get off the floor, Jonathan! Get off the floor!" As if I was falling on purpose. She put the tough in tough critic, but to her it was all love. Ma really was a New Yorker from the islands. She wanted me to be the most aggressive and strong kid out there, and she was perplexed when I couldn't just do it. She couldn't begin to know any of the things that were affecting me internally. It wasn't her fault; I just wouldn't share. I'd quietly cry in the back of the minivan as she lectured me on not being weak or afraid.

I picked up on the nuances of the game fairly quickly heading into seventh grade. I was playing basketball nonstop everyday. It was either the Y, playing with kids from our team, or kids at the middle school.

Playing ball for Coach Bora was on hold until the next summer, so the great Carlos of the YMCA took over my development. Carlos was a retired Boston Celtic player who lived in Naples. He would always pick me to be on his team and give me all types of pointers. He took interest in me in a way I needed when it came to basketball. I appreciate him so much for that. All day at school, I'd think about being on his team and how we were going to win.

Coach Carlos played the game the right way and made sure I did too. If I stood around, just wanting to score, he wouldn't hesitate to let me know that I couldn't play that way. He instilled a hard-working team player approach in me day after day. Back door cuts, screening to get free, moving without the ball, Iverson cuts, L cuts, give and go's, and so much more I learned playing alongside Carlos.

Playing basketball or thinking about basketball every moment of every day for the entirety of my seventh- and eighth-grade years, I started to pass other kids in terms of skill. Credit to Coach Carlos and the Estero Airforce. To my surprise, kids at school wanted to hoop and hang out with me. I noticed basketball worked better than class clowning, so I gave up the jokes. The combination of youth group and basketball muffled my insecurities to a low volume static, but they were still there whenever I didn't do as great as I wanted. My focus was the fact that I had more friends than ever and kids around me gave me respect.

When Coach Mark retired after my eighth-grade year, Coach Bora formed his own AAU team. We were now the Estero Elite. And a force to be reckoned with. At this point, I was one of the best players on the team and was falling madly in love with the game. We placed second in the USSSA Nationals Southeast Region the summer before high school.

That summer was also significant because through basketball I was able to meet Jeffercy, Jeremiah, and Arcaim.

We met at an inner-city hoops league. In a matter of days, we were all tight. The four musketeers. We always played until literal utter exhaustion, challenging each other to get better. They'd always be at my place, and Ma took them as her own. It was a brotherhood like I hadn't experienced up until then.

THE POTENTIAL OF PROMISE

By the time freshman year at Baron Collier High School started, I was a bona fide hooper. Playing ball with my bros all summer and also with Coach Bora leveled up my confidence, desire to be aggressive, and skill. Ma was proud. I'd even get some love from a few people around town. I enjoyed my little bit of fame. I played basketball because I loved the game, but I also thrived off what it brought me. Friendship, attention, a facade of peace. My aspiration was varsity basketball and not a thought past it. Never once did I think the NBA or even college basketball was in my future.

I killed it on the freshman team. Even though I was one of maybe two or three black kids on the team, I felt secure in my peer group with my fellow ballers. Not so much with my classmates. The remembrance of the disaster that was my elementary and middle school experience kept me up at night.

Basketball was easy. But basketball was after school, and the season didn't start until the middle of the school year. From 8 a.m. to 3 p.m., in my mind I was a nobody trying to put my best foot forward. I remember laying out an outfit the night before the first day that, to me, was perfect to catch a few eyes. Believe it or not, I once wore a red rhinestone belt. Even half-tucked in my shirt to show it off. I was so self-conscious about whether kids would think it was cool or think I was trying too hard. By the end of the day after a few side-eyes, I untucked my shirt to fully cover the belt.

In class, I was asked a question based on my appearance. "Are you from Ethiopia?" I was rail thin with dark skin and cheekbones as high as I was tall. I found myself laughing along while gritting from the sting. Behind the scenes, I was obsessively researching protein shakes and dietary supplements that could help me quickly put on weight. I remember ordering a product called Russian Bear that called for mixing the powder in a gallon of whole milk and drinking it in one day. A week in, I was sick, and Ma said she couldn't afford a gallon of milk every day. I also remember taking amino acid pills. One day after a workout, a coach saw me taking some at the water fountain and asked if I knew what they were or the proper way to use them. I didn't. I just didn't want to be called Ethiopian.

On the freshman ball team, we were all athletes, in the same grade, wanting to play our best no matter our color. And I was the man. I won team MVP at the closing of the season and was sure I'd play for varsity as a sophomore. With another summer of hooping with the bros and playing for Coach Bora coming up, I'd be more than ready. Suiting up alongside the guys I had looked up to my entire freshman year. Excited was an understatement. But nothing could prepare me for what I was about to endure.

Being the only sophomore and one of two black players on the varsity team was tough. The occasional hazing wasn't something I expected or was prepared for. One time they tried to make off with my pants while we were on an elevator. Naively and pridefully, I wanted to be celebrated for how good I was. They wanted to prove that I wasn't as good as I thought. They won. I went from averaging about twenty points a game my freshman year to less than four points my sophomore year.

Following my sophomore season and heading into the summer, a friend of mine suggested that I go to some workouts at the International School of Broward in Hollywood, Florida, about two hours away from Naples. Me and buddies Jeff and Jeremiah went to check out what all the hype was about. We loved the intensity of the workouts and found ourselves begging my mom's friend Ron to drive us to Hollywood each weekend.

The coaches saw my raw talent and promised me they could provide the training I needed to go the NBA. Those three letters were the farthest thing from my mind. They said I had the height and the potential, and they knew the pathway to get there. I was sold pretty quickly on college ball. The thought of getting out of Naples and us all playing for the same school brought back some of the excitement I'd lost.

The only question was, "What would our parents say?" I remember the deciding conversation I had with Ma. We were driving in the minivan. Jacob was with us. Ma told me that the choice was mine. If I wanted to go and swore to work hard, she would do whatever it took to make it happen. Jacob wasn't going to stay silent. "Why do you think it's going to be any different over there?" he blurted out.

"Wha-what are you talking about?" I replied, craning my neck toward the front seat so I could hear him better.

"Like, you suck here, so you'll just suck there too."

He might as well have buried a knife in my back, complete with several revolutions of turns and deeper jabs. Like any lil' bro, I wanted his approval.

Sometimes I wonder if he'd said something like, "You're going to be great out there," what that would have done for me. Would hearing words of encouragement have ignited a spark of self-belief? Would it have pushed me out of my vortex of insecurity? Maybe. In Jacob's defense, there's no way he could have known the depth of my insecurities. I'm sure his comment wasn't totally malicious.

Mom piped up immediately. "Jacob, shut your mouth. You don't know what you're talking about."

I didn't say a word the rest of the drive home. Ma blasted Gospel radio. Jacob tuned into his phone. I stared out the window at nothing. My body was calm, limbs still, head almost scraping the ceiling of the car. *What if he's right? What if I do just suck?*

"Well, we gone find out," I said to myself, "because I'm going!"

CHAPTER 3

GROWING PAINS

THE GYM IN HOLLYWOOD always stank of sweat-drenched teenagers and funky tennis shoes. I'd spent so many hours there over the summer with Jeffercy and Jeremiah. But when school started in the fall, I ended up attending alone, the only one able to convince his mother to let him go to a new high school two hours from home.

"You all make me sick!" was Coach Johnny's go-to. His voice soared over the noise of squeaky sneakers on the polished wooden floor. I'd hear his voice echo in my sleep. "What are we going to do with yawl sorry behinds?"

And that was just practice. You can only imagine the games.

Coach Johnny and his son/assistant, Jamal, were unlike any coaches I'd ever met. You might even call them mean. From the moment we set foot in the gym that summer, they meant business. Save the small talk and smiles for later. They would give us drills to run again and again and again. They would nit-pick every movement with comments that, if you weren't used to them, would have you crying mid-crossover. Once you'd get the drill down, you'd feel so accomplished. Then Coach would hit you with a "Okay, do it again!" Nothing was ever enough. He had a knack for breaking us players down, but he seemed to forget to build us back up. And yet we showed up, workout after workout. I relished it, despite the aggressive brand of coaching. The work and the grind were exciting, with no bright lights to expose my insecurities.

When Coach Johnny and Jamal first met me, they saw a little hard work and off to the NBA. But that's not what I saw. I was still in mental recovery from my sophomore season in Naples. Actually, I needed recovery long before I met my new teammates that year. I still didn't see value in me just being me. Trying to be someone people wanted still weighed heavy on my heart and a few buckets didn't change much. But this was a new start. A way to shake off the dust and build my confidence back to where it had been freshman year.

Remember Ron from the summer? What a trooper! He drove me from Naples to Hollywood most of my first year at ISB. It was almost an hour and forty-five-minute drive each way, every day. I'd wake up at 5:00 a.m., shower, get ready, and be at school by 7:30. Ron would wait for me after school to get out of practice around 9:30. I'd attempt my homework on the way back to Naples, get home sometime after 11:00 p.m., sleep, and do it all over again the next day. Weekends were to chill and hoop with the guys. Eventually, Ron got a job at a Publix near the school and rented a tiny apartment for us to stay at during the week, and we'd drive back to Naples only for the weekends. Ron was such a great help, I have to tell his story.

Ron met my mom at church. He came to live with us, and they dated for a few years, including my time at ISB onward. Ron was the man! He was rough around the edges but a sweet and endearing guy all the same.

Ron loved playing basketball and took a particular interest in me over my brothers because of it. His goal was to help me get some meat on my bones. That whole time I was drinking Russian Bear and taking amino acids, Ron was there. We'd hit the legendary local YMCA where I'd hoop with Carlos and do bicep and tricep curls, work on our shoulders, and get in some weighted squats as often as we could. It honestly didn't help much. I was still at least twenty to thirty pounds lighter than most of the kids I played with.

Ron would YouTube dribbling and other drills and work with me on them. Once he spent money I knew he didn't have on a pair of moon shoes for me that were supposed to increase your vertical jump. Yeah, they didn't work. I looked ridiculous running around the Y in them, but it showed he cared. Ron was there for me all through middle school and freshman year, but also for my downhill sophomore season. He understood there was a disconnect between the player he could see with his own two eyes and the player I felt I was in my mind. He'd say stuff like, "You're better than you think you are." He was always trying to encourage me to stop taking everything so seriously and just have fun.

THE PRESSURE HEIGHTENS

With games not far off as the school year progressed, we were all work and no fun. Coach Johnny and Jamal weren't completely crazy, but they were close. They made us do things they knew would push us to the very edge of giving up. And they taunted us the whole way there. Like when they made us run 17s until everyone on the team made the time. Including guards, bigs, and all. I don't even have to explain what 17s are—17 of anything that involves running is too many. But it wasn't in vain. The hard work showed and the coaches were excited about the championship season they believed was already ours with the squad we had. Nate, Tyreke, Joe. Most importantly me. I excelled in practice so much that the thought of me clamming up in a game never crossed their minds, I'm sure.

The only thing left to do was suit up and play.

I remember going into the first game of my junior season, trying to squash the pressure of the moment.

"It's just a game," I said, splashing cold water on my face. "Just treat it like a workout."

But it wasn't a workout. And the more I couldn't lie to my face, the more I began to panic. Thoughts of the coaches, teammates, and people I loved thinking maybe I wasn't who they thought I was.

What would Ron think after he'd spent so much time on me?

Would I disappoint Ma?

Would Jacob be right all along?

That evening I played afraid and timid. I secretly paid more attention to defense. I ran around distracted like I had other things on my mind. Which was true. On the bright side . . . we all did. Turns out we were all feeling the pressure of expectations and wanting to make everyone around us proud. So it wasn't obvious that I was struggling in a way more profound than just season-opener butterflies. Coach Johnny and Jamal were furious and lectured us on toughness as we ran 17 times back and forth between the lines.

With a chance to redeem ourselves fast approaching, the players came together and decided we were better than our first flop. Even though the start to the season mirrored my sophomore year, my teammates were different. Me, Tyreke, Nate, and Joe, we cared for one another. We bounced back in the second game, and to my surprise I played really well. So did my teammates. Maybe it was the feeling of being there for each other that made it easier to block out the noise.

The rest of my junior year season was chaotically up and down. I'd have a great game scoring twenty and then turn around and wet the bed. Feeling good about myself and then wanting to get as far away from myself as possible. The sensation I would have in my hands and forehead sometimes felt like an out-of-body experience. Some games would end with Ma and Ron being so excited about my future and others would end like this.

Mom: "What are you doing out there, Jonathan?"

Ron: "Yeah, man, I mean, what was going through your mind when you saw the lane was open? What's the hesitation?"

Mom: "You have to be aggressive, Jonathan! You were aggressive last game. Help me understand."

Ron: "She's right. These guys are shorter than you. Don't look for someone else to score when you've shown that you can score. If you see it, take it. Dunk on them. Get yours, Jonathan. No one else is going to do it for you."

I had one of two responses: complete silence, or letting out an emotional, frustrated, "I know. I know. I'm trying!" as tears swelled my eyes.

I had similar conversations with Coach Johnny and Jamal and even my teammates, but I wouldn't cry in front of them.

The problem was my mind. Good games would reinforce

that I was in control and could be what everyone wanted and liked. Bad ones would peel back all the progress.

We closed a mediocre season in defeat, but at least I showed some life from the previous year. I wasn't a complete train wreck. My family, coaches, and teammates expected me to play well and were disappointed when I didn't. That's progress. With the summer coming and the same group in sight, there was much to look forward to.

THINGS START LOOKING UP

It's hard to know who you are when you're constantly changing. For me, change came all at once, with location, mentality, and physical stature. I was back in Naples with my boys, and they were amazed at how tall I'd grown. I never had time to settle into any one size because I was continually inching toward the sky. My knees, back, and feet were always sore. Ma would joke that it was imperative that I make it to the NBA so I could pay her back for all the shopping she had to do for me as I outpaced my brothers.

I remember going to the doctor that summer, because the pain in my feet and knees was so prevalent. With an X-ray pinned to the wall, the doctor blared in excitement that my growth plates were WIDE open.

Sensing the confusion in my blank stare, the doctor broke it down into plain speak, "You are going to be seven feet tall and wear a size 17 shoe."

"No way," I replied. I couldn't picture myself at that size.

Already 6′6″, my knobby knees jutted off the end of the table as I looked at my size 14 feet, pondering the player I'd be at Kevin Durant's height. Hearing the news, you'd think the doctor had just told Ron and Coach Johnny they'd won the lotto. With my evolving capabilities on the court and a promising diagnosis, their eyes were set on the big leagues. I started getting excited too.

I took on AAU summer ball with a vengeance. I had started working with a trainer in Naples by the name of Akii. He spotted me at a local game and promised he could help take me to the next level. Working with him a couple times a week and playing ball on the summer circuit with Coach Johnny and Jamal, I started to make waves at tournaments around the country. Finishing up the Bob Gibbons tournament of Champions in Atlanta, national evaluators were talking about me. One wrote:

> "Easily the biggest revelation of the day came from the first game of the day. Isaac, a slight 6-foot-6 wing with lengthy arms, came out firing against the Upward Stars. Isaac, a confident shooter, made three long-range shots, including one from well past the line. Isaac competed on defense, was active the entire game and showed impressive mobility."[3]

Shortly after, another wrote this about my performance in the 16U Best of the South All Tournament:

> "He's very thin, long and skilled . . . Isaac has his own style, which includes above-average quickness despite his lack of muscle and a mechanically sound jump shot to the three-point line. He also handles and passes pretty well, and hopefully as he gains weight he'll become more athletic. Regardless, at 6-8 he's plenty tall to be a stretch four, and the Hollywood (Fla.) International School of Broward product will be a high-major mainstay for the remainder of his recruitment."

The wind was at my back and success was going to my head, but I still never expected what came next. Coach Johnny pulled me aside one day and told me a college coach was interested in coming to see me work out. I didn't believe him.

THE ONES WHO TOOK A CHANCE

The story goes that Coach Leonard Hamilton of Florida State University told the assistant coach, Coach Dennis Gates, to fly down and meet with me. Coach Johnny had given them his word that he had a kid they couldn't afford not to jump on early.

I'd never even thought about college before. And as far as ball goes, my ranking wasn't super impressive. I think at the time I was ranked 144th in the Rival's Top 150 spots for the class of 2016. Nothing to brag about. But what do you know? Coach Gates was on his way.

I remember being so nervous waiting for him to show up. But as I got moving on the court, it was just me and the ball. Comfortable, like being home. That happened in the best of games. Like for a moment in time, everything just clicked. There was no need to think about anything outside of the lines. Halfway through, I had forgotten that Coach Gates, with his shiny, glistening head, was even there. I was in my groove burying shot after shot behind the three-point line.

Dripping in sweat, I was hesitant to shake Coach's hand after the workout. Even though it went great, it felt cringey to initiate the awkward song and dance of introducing myself. Questions like, *What are we going to talk about? What does he want from me? And what did he think of the workout?* filleted my gut. I'd much preferred to skip the meet and greet and get his remarks in the mail.

Coach Gates is a good-looking dude. He had a great smile. His voice was strong and endearing and his personality cool and confident, the ideal recruiter. One of the first things he said to me when the workout was over was, "Young man, I want to offer you a scholarship. And I want to let you know that although they don't know who you are right now, the world will know who you are. I'm telling you, I can see you being in the top five players in the country in your graduating class."

He must have been speaking a different language by the look on my face. I didn't know what to say.

"Give us a chance to help you develop," he continued, without missing a beat. "This is just the beginning, and I want our relationship to be more than just basketball. Ultimately, I want you to understand that one day, your name is going to get called." *Okay. Now this brother is speaking blasphemies.* "Called by who?" I should have interjected. But I knew what he meant.

"Wow, well, um, cool, Coach," I responded, following up with a laugh and a sheepish grin. I had no training on how to correctly respond to being offered a scholarship. Pretty soon, Coach was on a plane back to Tallahassee telling Coach Hamilton, "This kid is a pro. Isaac has the potential to be the best player in the country. I don't care who we've offered a scholarship to or who we're looking at. I'm offering this kid one."

Coach Johnny reassured me that I'd have every major college coach in the country beating down my door in just a matter of time. I didn't believe him then either.

Coach Gates wasted no time wanting to know every detail of my background. But he did it in creative ways. His questions helped me to know myself better. In one phone conversation we had, he asked me this:

"If you got drafted today and you got an invite to the green room, who would you want to sit at your table?"

I kid you not, I had no idea what the "green room" was. Coach Gates explained that on draft night, most of the projected lottery picks sat with their representation, coaches, and loved ones right in front of the stage known as the green room. I needed clarity on lottery picks too.

"You get to choose about eight people," Coach Gates said. "Who would you want to sit at the table with you?"

The first person was easy. "Ma, of course." Pause. "Maybe my Pops too."

"Okay, who else?"

"I don't know, Coach. My family, I guess."

Coach Gates casually asked, "So, why'd you hesitate on your dad being there?"

"I don't know, man." I said with the fraction of bass I had. Of course, I knew.

The man sensed my discomfort and eased up. "Okay, what's your dad's name, Jonathan?"

"Jacob." Silence. *I hoped all college recruiting wasn't a barrage of personal questions. This is so weird.* But then I added: "I don't really talk to my dad that much, Coach."

"Okay, young fella. This is what we're going to do. Tell me more about your dad. Tell me your memories about him. Tell me about his life."

So, I told him about Superman. Followed by the McDonald's, the split, the move, and the progressive lack of relationship I had with Pops at this point. He asked how I thought it affected me, but Coach Gates wasn't getting much out of me past "I'm good" and "Don't really think about it at all."

"What's your middle name?" Coach Gates asked toward

the end of the conversation. "Judah. I'm Jonathan Judah Isaac."

He blurted out, "Man, do you realize your dad's name, Jacob, and your middle name, Judah, is biblical? Judah is Jacob's fourth son."

"That's pretty cool!"

"Man, I'm going to call you Judah from now on."

I was okay with that. He'd be the only one to call me by that name, for now. I started to love it. I began to redefine myself under Judah, though that new me wouldn't manifest until years later.

My conversation with Coach Gates ended where it began: the green room. "The day you get drafted," he told me, "We're going to make sure that your relationship with your dad is restored and you feel comfortable enough to have him at your table."

From then on, Coach Gates and I rarely talked about my recruitment process or decision. We talked about life, girls, my dreams and aspirations. It was clear to me that he was interested in me as a person. It was uncomfortable, but nice. We'd talk several times a day at times. Ma hated it. Every time she saw me on the phone, she'd ask who I was talking to.

"Coach Gates, Ma."

"Get off the phone, Jonathan."

"But, Ma—"

"Get off the phone!"

Ma was happy for me but wanted me to explore all my options and not settle for the first D1 offer. She didn't see Florida State as a big-name basketball school.

Heading into my senior season I was still under the radar. With FSU being the biggest school to reach out, I was eager to kill it that season and go with the best option available. It didn't turn out quite as I'd hoped. I had a great year with plenty more ups than downs. I led the state in points, averaging twenty-nine-and-a-half points, nine boards, and three blocks. But the year ended without any bigger schools recruiting me.

When the time came to make a decision, I was still slightly young for college and behind on major physical development. We decided that a post grad year of high school would be best for me. That's right. Me, Ma, and Coach Gates. Without even a verbal commitment that I'd attend FSU after my fifth year, Coach Gates dished out advice even though he and Coach Hamilton would have gladly taken me that year.

I enrolled in IMG Academy the spring of 2015 and lived on campus the summer leading up to the school year. The school was big time, having trained and coached numerous Olympians and professional athletes. It was like a college. I began the summer circuit playing for Each 1 Teach 1 in Nike's Elite Youth Basketball League (EYBL), the highest level of high school basketball. I'd leave IMG for tournaments on the weekend.

A FALSE SENSE OF CONFIDENCE

Stepping onto IMG campus, I was as big headed as ever. Knowing how I'd struggled with self-esteem in the past, I should have been ashamed of myself for the inflated ego. But all the love I was getting didn't make it easy. People whispering about who I was started to become my normal. For the first time, I was actually cool. Girls liked me, and guys wanted to be me. Walking into gyms feeling "less than" was past tense. I was no longer worried about not getting people's love, attention, or approval. Now I was worried about keeping it. That would present its own problems, but for the moment I was full speed ahead basking in every compliment and news clipping on my way to the big leagues.

I continued building on the faulty grounds of validation into the summer as college offers began to roll in. Head Coach John Mahoney would rattle off a new list of schools every day, either offering a scholarship or wanting to come on campus to talk with me. I entered a world I had no idea existed. One day Miami was coming to see me practice. The next day Florida wanted to have lunch. One night, I had back-to-back phone calls from PITT, Louisville, and Kentucky, all offering scholarships. My Instagram and Twitter followers hit the thousands as clips of my games landed on YouTube. Coach Gates was there for it all. Without pressuring me, he listened as I expressed a desire to throw my phone in the campus lake, as if I didn't enjoy every second of this.

The pressure was on for me to pick a school. Most guys in my class had already committed to their school of choice, and I was getting pulled in every direction. Ma wanted me to go to Kentucky as they put the most players in the league at the time. Ron had been a lifelong Kansas fan, so he dropped some hints without being too pushy. Coach Mahoney would swear to this day that he wasn't pulling for me to go to Michigan, but who are we kidding? He loved them. Our team ran their system, and he was the only reason they were on my list. My E1T1 coach had the in with LSU and had no shame about being pushy. And there were still other schools on the list. Florida, Miami, Stanford, Wake Forest, and a couple others. I didn't know what I was doing, but I knew my heart was with Coach Gates at Florida State. I wanted a school that wouldn't just see me as a basketball player. Coach Gates understood my talent but also my struggle. Still, I procrastinated, knowing my decision would leave a lot of folks disappointed.

I remember texting Coach Gates,

Me: "You're not mad that I haven't committed yet?"

Coach: "Not at all. You'll do it when you're ready."

Me: "So that's it?

Coach: "Yep. This, me and you, is beyond basketball. If you want to go somewhere else, go ahead and go somewhere else. I understand. Know that I will always be the same person I am now for you. Always!"

I made my decision after reading that text and walked into Coach Mahoney's office to tell him the news. He had one stipulation. "You've got to call these schools back. If you don't want to go there, you have to let them know. Say something like, 'Coach, I appreciate the interest you've shown in me, but I don't think it's the right fit for me.'"

I puckered my brows. "Say what now?!"

"I know it's awkward and uncomfortable, but you have to do it. It's respectable. Just be yourself. Let's get the list together and start making calls."

Just be yourself. Sure.

The first phone call sucked. My voice trembled, not knowing how the coach was going to react. Every call got easier and pulled me closer to where I knew I belonged.

A day or two later I called Coach Gates and asked him to help me edit the announcement I'd make on Twitter. And on July 6, 2015, I posted:

"So much help and guidance to get to this point! But in making my own decision I've closed my recruitment and commit to FSU!! #GoNoles."

Before heading off to FSU, I was invited to some big-time events. Like playing on the EYBL's Select Team in the Bahamas. Also, the Jordan Brand All-American Game and the USA Junior National Select Team. The prime time Peach Jam tournament capped off the AAU season, with the winner being EYBL champs.

For the first game of the Peach Jam tournament, my trainer Akii had a front row seat to witness my terrible performance. After the game, he handed me two books. One was called *Relentless: From Good to Great to Unstoppable* by Tim Grover, and the other was *Not a Fan: Becoming a Completely Committed Follower of Jesus* by Kyle Idleman. I read through a bit of *Relentless* but didn't touch *Not a Fan.* Since he'd started working out with me, he'd casually insert Jesus stuff into texts or invite me to Bible studies. Unresponsive, I kept things nonspiritual. I just wanted him to train me.

Akii texted me later that night, "Keep your head up. Check out those books I gave you, especially *Relentless*. It talks about the mindset of being an elite athlete."

I read his last few words carefully. *The mindset of an elite athlete*. I knew everyone was expecting me to be just that. Some of the prestigious events I got invited to hadn't gone as I'd planned. The foundation of basing my worth off of people's opinions was beginning to shake. I feared losing all the fame I had gained.

In a frustrated text back to Akii, I wrote, "I don't get it. I don't know why everyone thinks I'm so good. What do they see in me?" My mind was up to its old tricks.

Akii was a great encourager. Thank God. He replied back with a long text that boosted my spirits. I saw him the next day and said, "My bad about last night. I was tripping. I'm good now."

As the tournament progressed, I got back to the elite athlete I was used to. Unfortunately, we lost to Chris Paul's CP3 team in the quarter finals. After the game I sat alone on the bleachers with my head in my hands. I felt a tap on the shoulder and looked up. There was Chris Paul himself. He asked what my name was, and after I told him, he stated with confidence that I should keep my head up because I'd be playing with him in the NBA in two years. And just like that, he walked off.

I'll never forget it.

REUNITING WITH SUPERMAN

Coach Gates and I still had talks about home, and he was still on me about what my relationship with my Pops was like. It wasn't necessarily broken. Out of touch might be a better way to put it. Unbeknownst to me, Coach Gates had sent my Pops a letter introducing himself. In their first conversation, Coach Gates said, "Mr. Isaac, with all due respect, Jonathan is going to be with us at Florida State. Obviously, I don't want the first time you and I meet to be when he graduates."

Coach Gates arranged for Pops to come to the Jordan Brand game, which was right in New York at the Barclays Center. Coach made plans for the three of us to hang for a bit before I had to fly back to Florida the next day.

It was far from my best game. Definitely not my worst either. I had eight points, six rebounds, and one blocked shot in eighteen minutes of play. There may have been a few airballs in the mix. As the final buzzer sounded and I jogged back to the locker room, I remember not knowing what I was supposed to do next. *Were Pops and I supposed to meet up now? Do I call him? Is he supposed to call me?* I felt like maybe it just wasn't meant to be. Turns out my dad went to the wrong arena. *How in the world could we have messed this up so badly?*

Fortunately, Pops met me at LaGuardia Airport the next morning. I pulled up to the passenger drop-off curb, collected my bags, looked around the crowded walkway for a few seconds, and then I saw him. The first thing I noticed was that he looked older. Streaks of white salted the peach fuzz on his cheeks and his neatly trimmed mustache. He was holding on to the bit of hair he had left on his head and was dressed for church. Oh, and I was a head taller than him. Freaked me out. He was still Superman, though.

We hugged, not like father and son who were reunited after six some years, but like father and son who hadn't seen each other for a summer because I'd been at camp or something. There were no tears or I miss yous. I wasn't mad at him. It was just Pops. He was here. And so was I.

We grabbed some food, and I remember showing him a picture of the girl I was hanging out with at the time. Pops looked at her and said, "Ooh, she might be a little fast for you." That's Pops.

We talked basketball. I answered his questions about the Jordan Brand and what was to come. I enjoyed the simplicity of the conversation, actually the longest we'd had in a long time. He gave me some money before we hugged, and he said goodbye the way I'd always remembered it. "Love you, love you." And then I checked in for my flight.

I'd get the opportunity to see Pops when I played at the Barclays Center four more times.

Graduating IMG, I was the number-one ranked player in the state of Florida, number-three small forward in the country, and number-twelve overall by 247Sports.com; number-nine overall by ESPN.com; number-five overall by scout.com.

Coach Gates was right; I was now a top five player in my class. He must be a prophet. As exciting as it was, there wasn't much time to celebrate. I was on my way to FSU, leaving behind Coach Mahoney and my two best friends from the team, Aleem and Meech. Hopefully I was prepared for the new set of challenges that awaited me, as I became "Big Man on Campus."

CHAPTER 4

PANIC IN PARADISE

FLORIDA STATE SUMMER SCHOOL was underway. It wasn't my fault I sent my new teammate Mfiondu Kabengele ("Fi") limping to the trainer's room with a sprained ankle on the team's first open gym. Here's how it went down.

I had heard that Fi was talking straight lunacy days before I arrived on campus. He told Coach Gates and the other guys that he had watched all my highlights and wasn't concerned in the least about who was better, and he'd prove it the second my kicks hit the hardwood. "This kid Isaac's got nothing on me!" he had boasted to Coach. "He's too thin!"

We were set to play fives late in the evening on that first day. Everyone was anticipating the matchup with all the trash talk coming from Fi. I never was the type of player to talk trash, as afraid of eating my own words as I was of hurting someone's feelings. I'd never seen Fi play or heard of him, but I was confident I'd be able to handle my own.

"Y'all make sure there's no arguing over fouls and no bs," Coach Gates told us before leaving us to our own devices. "Play some hard up and down scrimmages. You guys know how we do."

We quickly broke into teams, all of us wanting to show each other we had game. I remember Fi staring me down, determined to show me up. "Let's go," he taunted, minimizing my personal space so I could see his nostrils flare. "You and me."

I shrugged my shoulders as we checked up, "Let's just hoop, bro."

But dude wouldn't let up. I actually liked that about Fi right off the bat. He believed in himself and was bent on showing it. A couple possessions in, I had the ball. Fi overzealously tried to strip, and with a right to left cross, I was at the basket, and that was Fi's last play of the night. He rolled his ankle from the shift, and from that day on, I had Fi's respect. The confrontation brought out the best in us, and we grew as friends.

Mfiondu's swollen ankle aside, that night was really big for me. It put everyone on notice and helped me take my first deep breath since being on campus. I could work out and play pickup all day long without fraying my nerves. This renewed confidence pushed my fears about the impending season to the back of my mind. Day after day, my teammates and I balled. And I kept on rolling.

AN UNWELCOME VISITOR

The jump to basketball recognition on campus was similar to my physical growth spurts. I wasn't ready for either one. Sure, I was a hometown hero down south and was used to a bit of praise. But this was Tallahassee. It felt strange to be a big deal. The constant handshakes and high fives and pats on the back, and even the string of comments about me going top ten felt like high school recruitment all over again. That all too familiar whisper of fear and doubt haunted me, even as I bathed in the glory, walking through campus with my head high.

But this was only summer school. The season was still months away. I had time to enjoy getting to know my teammates and learn my surroundings. Me, CJ, Trent, Travis, and Fi were the new kids. Me and CJ were roommates. Our relationship catapulted one night while we played video games. Gospel music, courtesy of yours truly, played in the background.

CJ went quiet as Marvin Sapp crooned, "Never would have made it, never could have made it, without you." I noticed a tear glide down CJ's cheek.

"You okay, bro?" I asked.

"This song was one of my grandmother's favorites," CJ quietly answered. "She passed away right before I got to college."

We sat in silence, rocking back and forth while Marvin blessed the speakers. From that moment on, CJ and I became more than teammates. We became friends. Over the next year, he would see me at my best and at my worst. And through it all, he never left my side.

All us teammates gelled quickly. Before our real semester officially started, it was tradition for the players to work the school's youth basketball camp as refs and coaches to put some money in our pockets. Kids of all ages showed up, from teens to as young as eight. I was excited to get paid to goof off with them and block their shots. I didn't expect having a breakdown to be a part of the experience.

The camp lasted a week. Every day it got a bit harder to enjoy. It doesn't sound like a bad thing, but everyone knew who I was. All the kids talked about was Florida State getting back to the tournament after a disappointing NIT showing. To them, I was the chosen one for this goal. It felt like all eyes were on me. With each passing day, I grew more tense and retreated into my head. By the last day, it was like I wasn't there.

I can vividly picture the moment when, in the midst of pizza and juice boxes, I started feeling my breath get shallow. I walked out the nearest door to get some air as tears welled in my eyes. Just me and a forklift on a loading dock. The dam burst. I started crying out everything I'd been holding in.

I barely heard the concerned voices of my teammates who found me out in the loading area.

"Yo, you alright bro?"

"JI, you good?"

"Hey, J, what happened?"

Finally, a voice broke through the weepy haze. "Y'all go ahead. Let me talk to him." It was Coach Gates.

I could barely gasp for breath, let alone spill out a complete sentence explaining to Coach what was up. But this wasn't his first rodeo with me. He sat down, a few inches away, without saying a word. Finally, my breath stabilized. I dried the runway stream from my cheeks. I was okay.

"I don't get it. It's just, it's just," I stammered. "Everybody's saying all these things."

"Who, Judah," Coach nudged. "Who's everybody? And what things?"

"It seems like everybody! Saying I'll be one and done. A millionaire lottery pick. The reason we make the tourney this year."

Coach nodded and put his arm on my back.

"I'm not who they think I am," I murmured, dropping my head.

"I've always told you a lot of things are going to come with your success. And this is one of them. People are going to talk. They always do. It's because of what they see in you. You just gotta be you, do you. You're okay. We're all here for you. You got this."

I listened to Coach, nodding and trying to soak in what he was telling me. "You're good, Judah," he'd tell me over and over every time I'd try to make the case that I was a fraud.

I couldn't articulate it to Coach Gates that day on the loading dock. What he didn't understand was that in my mind, being me *was* the problem. I saw every great thing I'd done as something outside of me and every failure and weakness as who I was. This was why I craved the attention and accolades, and why I'd crumble under the weight of my accusatory whispers that I was a fraud and a failure. The truth was, I was exactly who they thought I was. It was me who couldn't believe it.

Letting out all the tears and talking with Coach brought me back to ground zero. Enjoying the people around me, new faces and old, and killing in pickup. My teammates were still a bit concerned, but seeing me back to normal reassured them I was okay.

FORESHOCKS

Talk of the upcoming season was in everyone's mouth. No more pickup games. It was time for real practice. The mood instantly shifted. The fluffy smiles and laughter of the coaches turned to yells and piercing whistles. Practice was hit or miss for me early on. I'd either be relaxed and sharp, showing off exactly the player I was, or anxious, head in the fog a million miles away. As we inched toward the season, I flip-flopped between the two states until something I'd never experienced before happened.

One morning, I sat down with my plate of grits and tater tots in the Suwannee Room, where we all had breakfast most mornings on campus. Over breakfast, we'd make jokes about the coaches, talk about how tired we were, how much work we had, and lastly, how lit the season was going to be. Chuckling as usual, I put a spoon of grits to my mouth, and that's all I remember of clear consciousness. An out-of-body feeling swept over me like *The Matrix*. Out of nowhere, the scene around me faded to a dull whisper. On one hand, I was conscious of sitting at the table eating breakfast with my teammates. On the other hand, I was paralyzed in a state of loading, as though the Wi-Fi went out in my brain. The sensation lasted a few seconds, which feels more like a few hours when you're in it, and it left me wondering if this is what it feels like to be drugged.

The feeling came on so quickly and so powerfully, I didn't have a chance to really register what had happened. I made sure no one noticed I was off, and thankfully, they were all still laughing about whoever said what. After that I didn't dwell on it too much. At all, really. I buried it with a litany of excuses. *I was dehydrated. I hadn't eaten dinner the night before. Maybe my asthma was manifesting in a weird way.* If it wasn't asthma, maybe it was stress. Deep inside I knew I was stressed about the season, but I didn't know anything about its effects, so I couldn't connect the dots. It was easier for me to brush it off rather than dig deeper into how I was feeling. And granted, I had been stressed plenty of times before, but I had never experienced this. For someone on the outside looking in, I had everything a young guy could want. I was living proof that we can hide something as serious as stress from others—and even from ourselves.

I tried to move forward and forget about it. But it happened a few more times and then began to occur routinely, a couple days a week. The second time I wondered if maybe it was the food (sorry, no offense, Suwannee Room). The third time I wondered if there was something seriously wrong with me. And every time after that, I expected its onset and handled it in silence.

A study published in the Journal of Zoology discovered that five days before an earthquake struck L'Aquila in Italy in 2009, 96% of male toads fled their breeding site area.[4] These toads could be on to something. While these little critters may be able to detect an approaching quake, God just didn't make us that way. You've probably heard of aftershocks, the little earthquakes that happen after a major one strikes. You may not know that some major earthquakes discharge foreshocks, smaller tremors that can occur hours or days before. But scientists don't know a foreshock is a foreshock until the actual major earthquake happens.

I think of the experience at the breakfast table as a foreshock that should have set off the alarms of something brewing deep under the surface. I coped by quieting the sirens. If you saw me on campus, you'd think I was more than fine. Being able to turn on the Jonathan Isaac charm that floated me through the day after having a panic attack for breakfast is a human phenomenon that we are all familiar with. I pretended to be the man. I smiled often. Got good grades. Had fun. Went out with my teammates and had success with the ladies, to keep it PG. It was dope. I looked unstoppable to the naked eye while riding the rollercoaster of my fragile identity in the shadows.

The earth's crust, in the form of tectonic plates, is constantly shifting. Sometimes these rocky plates get stuck at their edges. When enough pressure builds to overwhelm the friction, energy is released in the form of seismic waves. Boom, earthquake.

EARTHQUAKE!

I was in my learning specialist's office in the fall with my buddy CJ when the ground shook the first time. With our laptops open and a few books spread out, I leaned in as Lauren, our learning specialist, helped map out my assignments and track my progress. I was the type of student who'd get paralyzed in the pursuit of perfection. I couldn't write the first sentence of a paper because I believed what I had in mind wasn't up to Lauren's standard.

As me and CJ settled into our workflow, I mentioned to Lauren that I wasn't feeling well.

"Need anything?" she asked.

"Nah," I replied, and started typing away. It wasn't but a few minutes later when my fingers froze on the keyboard as I thought, *Not here! Not now*!

My chest tightened as panic spiked through my body. I began to hyperventilate. I tried inhaling but couldn't gulp enough air. The deeper I tried to breathe, the less oxygen there was to consume. Everything began to fade as my eyelids fluttered and my eyes rolled back. I caught a couple moments of CJ yelling, "Bro chill you okay!" as he shook my shoulders. And poor Lauren almost had an episode of her own out of fear and sympathy for me.

Then, blackness.

When I came to, I was lying on a stretcher that was way too small for me and had an oxygen mask fastened over my face. I had no idea what had happened. I could hear Lauren's voice, "Oh my God," though it sounded like she was in the next room. I blinked a few times and saw CJ's face in the far corner, his eyes swollen and red. A team of paramedics were huddled around me. Next thing I remember is being loaded into an ambulance. I removed the mask to ask what had happened.

"It seems like you passed out, buddy," a calm voice responded, as a cuff was fastened around my arm to check my blood pressure.

I lifted my head a few inches to look around. *Is that Amanda*? I was so confused. Amanda was the team's trainer and, to me, "Grandma." Not actually, but she had a soothing maturity about her. Hard to be around her and not feel calmer. She always told us what to do to stay healthy, so Grandma it was.

"Hey, JI, you okay? How you feeling?" she pleaded, her eyes shadowed with worry. Her obvious distress deepened my discomfort, not knowing what all the commotion was about.

By the time I got to the hospital and into a private room, Coach Gates had arrived. Amanda was there too. And CJ, of course, who had parked himself at the foot of my bed.

Despite passing out, I was in good spirits. It was like I didn't fully compute what passing out meant. Without hesitation, I reached for my phone, which was somehow still in my pocket, and clicked on SWV's hit "Weak," to liven the mood. Amanda and I shared a bond in the training room over old R&B.

"I get so weak in the knees
I can hardly speak (I do)
I lose all control (control)
And something takes over me (takes over me)"

CJ was confused, but Amanda chuckled. Coach Gates looked up from his phone and straight at me. "Oh yeah, you was definitely weak, Judah."

We all laughed.

"And what do you know about this song anyway? You weren't even thought of when the song came out," Coach teased.

I was released from the hospital the same day. Physically, nothing was wrong to warrant an admission. I was worried that word of my episode would get out and that people would talk. Coach Gates assured me that he'd handle it. He did. To this day, not even my family knows some of the things that went on during that time.

I was ready to keep moving as if nothing had happened, but the coaching and training staff were concerned and needed answers. The doctor who examined me ruled out asthma as a cause. Funny, a few weeks later, going in for an allergy work up, a pulmonologist would tell me my lungs were in excellent shape and I absolutely did not suffer from asthma, and, get this, probably never did. Turns out my history of asthmatic episodes were anxiety attacks thwarted by good old-fashioned Albuterol and belief.

When Amanda and I talked to the neurologist, he hit me with the mic drop: "I think you're fine. I don't think you passed out. I think you had an anxiety attack and made yourself pass out." Real awkward silence. "But that is just my opinion. I think we should monitor it and if it happens again, I'll see you then."

There's no way I forced myself to pass out, I told Amanda on our way out. That didn't make any sense to me. So I went back to hoop. I got back in my flow. It was as if every episode of breakdown was an emotional reset. For the time being, my mind was clear.

A PRIVATE EXPOSE

A month later, it happened again. This time, in anthropology class. CJ sat to my left, and another friend sat to my right. There were about three hundred students in the auditorium listening to a professor who was as boring as quarantine. She used a game called Kahoot! where we'd all race to select the right answer for points. I was actually enjoying it until suddenly, déjà vu.

I felt hot, like a surge of electricity went through my body. And as usual, everything around me slowly faded.

I closed my eyes and put my head back, trying to take deep breaths and control the fidgeting. But CJ knew what was going on

"Let's go," he whispered to me and my friend, trying to discretely collect our belongings.

The room tipped slowly from side to side as I walked up the aisle muttering what I intended to be "Excuse me." Our professor barked a demand to know where we were headed in the middle of a quiz, but we all just kept moving until we got outside. We could explain later.

CJ was telling me to breath and relax, while our friend looked on completely bewildered at what had just happened. I could tell CJ was concerned. Not in anything he said but in his eyes. He had these two incidents to contrast with the always cool hooper. Those two realities couldn't be farther apart.

I recovered. One second feeling like I was being chased,

and then I was calm, like I made the whole thing up. No hospital this time. Me and CJ made our way to the training room to see Amanda. Coach Gates met us, and we all sat down to debrief about what was happening to me.

"Do you remember what happened this time? How did it start?" Coach Gates asked.

"I just remember feeling increasingly hot and like an uncontainable energy over me."

"Were you anxious about anything? Did you have a test or something?" inquired Amanda.

"We were on this stupid Kahoot thing. But I was chill. It was actually fun. And then just didn't feel good."

Amanda nudged further. "I'm curious. Did your palms get real sweaty before it happened?"

My eyes widened. "Yeah! Honestly, I was sweating all over. It was hard to breathe too, like before."

"It sounds like you had another panic attack, J." Amanda pressed gently. "I don't know if you want to talk about it, but I think a lot of what's happening has to do with your mental state. I think you should talk to someone. There are so many resources here for you, and no one needs to know. What do you think?"

Amanda knowing the truth about my anxiety made me feel terrible about myself. So did the pitied look CJ had in his eyes. I found myself in the same place I'd been running from time after time. My weakness and inadequacy were brought to light. I hadn't yet figured out that no matter how high you build on a faulty foundation, it's only a matter of time until the façade collapses. The cat was out of the bag, at least with Coach Gates, Amanda, and CJ.

Heading into the season, I started seeing the team psychologist. Our first conversation went something like this. He asked, "Help me understand what's going on. You're a good-looking guy. I'm sure you don't have any problems with the girls. You've got a great smile and personality and are extremely talented. Where do you feel is the disconnect?"

I didn't trust him and frankly didn't know the answer he wanted to hear, so I didn't give him anything. But it made me think. *He was right! What the heck is the problem? Get past all the soft stuff and do what you do. Hoop! You've got everything anybody wants!* As the season started, I ditched my inhaler for a prescribed pill or two of Xanax before or during games and practices. Most times it would take the edge off, though not always. I balled out in our two preseason games and was excited for the real thing. The hype was real. FSU was making the tournament this year.

Around this time, Amanda invited me and CJ to her church. I hadn't been to church in a while but always knew it carried significance. In my mind, church was a way to look at the deeper things in life and progress to being a better person. I enjoyed the experience with

Amanda and CJ. The pastor was charismatic and easy to listen to. Knowing God didn't approve, I started feeling guilty about some of my late-night decisions, so I traded nights out to stay in and study or play video games. I even deleted all of the secular music off my phone to try and stay focused. A couple weeks into going to church, I was in a better place.

NOTHING STAYS PERFECT

The first couple games of the season went well. With no breakdowns, I was on the path to the season everyone expected. I was already high on NBA draft boards for the next year. I wouldn't call it a trigger but maybe a foreshadowing that not everything stays perfect.

One afternoon Amanda mentioned to me that things at the church weren't going well. Their pastor was on hiatus after being caught sleeping with a member of the congregation in reality TV fashion. I was furious. I swore I'd never step foot in her church again, or any church for that matter. I used him as an excuse to self-righteously explain my absence. Besides, I had to focus on hoop.

The team pressed on doing our thing. Playing with these guys felt natural. We were connected like a family. By the middle of the year, we had won fifteen out of sixteen games and were a top fifteen team in the country. I received a Freshman of the Week honors myself. That's not to say that I played great in every game, but I was managing.

As games got more meaningful, fears of letting the team down or forfeiting the league threatened to stall my progress and depress my performance. I got into a pattern of struggling in the first half of games and playing well in the second. It wasn't too noticeable in the first half of the season. But I could feel the unease in me grow and become harder to fake through.

Coach Gates started to realize and tried harder to keep me encouraged. Another coach, "CY," would constantly tell me I had no worries. That I could play with my eyes closed and put up twenty and ten. CY told me to just relax and be me. The second half of games I could do just that.

The twenty-minute intermission would reset my head and release my ability, but not in the way you'd expect. I'd usually break down in tears in a side room with Gates and Amanda. Like clockwork, I'd be super high strung before the game. Start it with mistakes and airballs, then begin to berate myself mentally for my performance and what everyone must be thinking. Come second half, I'd play to my ability, as if the first half hadn't even happened.

I'll never forget when second-half Jonathan showed up in our January 18 game against Notre Dame. After the game, Coach Hamilton was quoted as saying this about me, "He is gaining more confidence; he doesn't feel any pressure."[5] Which was true, and while it was probably my best game, he probably only remembers the second half. If you saw me in my halftime meeting with Amanda and

Coach Gates, you never would have believed I didn't "feel any pressure." You'd think I was a mess.

The Fighting Irish dominated the first half, making 71.4% of their shots from beyond the arc. I had six points. This was a big game, and everyone knew I had to be on for us to win. As usual, I was overwhelmed emotionally and couldn't stop the tears.

"Don't you see what this is?" Coach Gates prodded, his hands waving in the air. "You're a second-half player, Jonathan. C'mon. You know this by now. Trust me. You are okay. Your team is going to be okay. Get back out there and get your second wind!"

He was right. After the last tear fell, I muttered to myself, *Yeah. I am a second-half player. I am a fighter. I can do this.* And I rejoined my teammates.

We trailed Notre Dame 62-64 with 5:40 on the clock. I knocked a three, giving us a lead of one point. A defensive rebound turned into an outlet pass, to a layup for me, and a free throw from a foul. At three minutes left, we were up 70-65. Florida State fans were going berserk. Notre Dame tried to make one last push with under a minute left. They hit a three, and everything froze: We're up eighty-three to eighty, and I'm taking the ball out underneath our basket against their full-court pressure. In a split second I threw the ball in and it got intercepted. As the crowd gasped and another split second passed, I was blocking V.J. Beachem's layup attempt. With a few seconds left, the ball went straight to his teammate Bonzi Colson, and he tried to quickly lay the ball in on the other side of the hoop. Without thinking, I set my feet and blocked the layup as the final buzzer sounded. Florida State closed it out. I finished with twenty-three points, seventeen of them in the second half, and thirteen in the final six minutes. Oh, and a season high: seven blocks.

As the last quarter of the season raged on, half-time therapy sessions dwindled. I wasn't cured, but I had found a nice medium between battling the shipwrecking thoughts and allowing myself to feel them. I turned down the Xanax for good. I had gotten comfortable being in a good state, but I hadn't found a lasting peace.

Good news: We did what everyone projected. Maybe my worries were futile after all. We made it to the NCAA tournament and won our first game. For our second and my final game in the garnet and gold, we lost to Xavier at the Amway Center in Orlando. It was a crushing loss as we knew we were better than our performance, but it was over.

And in the blink of an eye, my top ten draft projection to the pros was front and center. Deep inside I knew what that meant: a new normal I didn't feel ready for. Or quite frankly, didn't want. I'd thought to myself: *With a summer to train and the big mental stumbling blocks out of the way, I'd have twice as good of a season at FSU next year.*

My mother had other plans. When we got back to the hotel after the loss to Xavier, Ma explained with sharp authority that I was going to play in the NBA the next season. "This is your last game. You're going in the draft."

Fueled by fear of what the next level called for, I clapped back, "No, I'm not." Boy did that open up a can of worms. Ma was furious, and without knowing where I was coming from, she had every right to be. She suspected the coaches were convincing me to stay another year.

To her relief, Coach Gates would refuse to welcome me back.

CHAPTER 5

MEMORIES OF A ROOKIE

"I HAVE TO COME BACK TO SCHOOL NEXT YEAR," I told Coach Gates.

He sighed, then swallowed hard. "You have to do what now, Judah?" he asked, even though he had definitely heard me the first time. "Explain why."

"I don't want to declare. I'm coming back to Florida State. With another year to train and being in a better space, I'll have a way better year next season," I stated, throwing a basketball up in the air and catching it over and over.

Coach Gates took a long look at me. As the silence grew, the muscles in his face unclenched. "You don't belong here anymore, Judah," he said with a chuckle. "You're going to be a top ten pick. There's no reason to stay. There's nothing left for you to do here. You're going to be able to create a legacy for your family out there. You're going. I will pack your bags myself."

The ball slipped out of my hand, rhythmically decelerating its pace until my outstretched leg caught it.

This was news. I expected Coach Gates to doubt my readiness and to cosign my reasoning. Even though a part of me was excited about the future, I just didn't want to say it. I wanted him to make the choice for me. But he couldn't. I had to.

DRAFT DECISIONS

Coach Gates and I put our heads together on the best way to announce the big decision, and we decided to film a video in the FSU gym. On Friday, March 24, 2017, with Ma by my side smiling sweetly at the camera, I posted the video on social media giving my thanks and goodbyes.

> "I've decided to enter the 2017 NBA draft. I'd like to thank all of Florida State for making my time here worthwhile. And a special thanks to all you fans and FSU's amazing staff. I've truly enjoyed my time here, and it's all because of you guys. I know this season didn't end as well as everyone expected, but I'm extremely proud of what this team accomplished. And I'm honored to be a part of the Seminole basketball family."

I was the second player in Florida State history to enter the draft after only one season. Malik Beasley was the first the year before. And for where I was slated to go in the draft, I could be the highest draft pick for State in some forty-seven years. I averaged a respectable twelve points, even though there was definitely more in me, and led the team in rebounding with eight a game. I also won Athlete of the Year for FSU Athletics. More than stats and awards, I loved the team. We had a lot of fun and grew into a real family in such a short time.

But it was over. And in its place, the fast-paced nature of the pre-draft process was here.

Coach had stacks of letters and packets from agents who were interested in representing me that he had tucked away in a drawer until it was time to make a decision. Smart guy. The checklist was pretty straight forward: pick an agent, finish the semester out at FSU, train somewhere for the summer, and get drafted. I liked the way Coach Gates went about the agent process. The ones that sent mail to the school and went through my coaches were on a "good" list. Anyone else trying to stop me on campus or hit me or my mom up on social media never even got a chance.

It felt good to be wanted. Especially when one of the agents courting me represented Lebron James. Maybe this meant I was ready. The process took a week of phone calls setting up meetings and another week of sit-down presentations with me, Ma, and FSU coaches. Ultimately, I chose Jeff Wechsler. He was confident in his work, precise, and direct. I was one step closer to the league.

I finished out the semester training with Akii on campus. I was so dialed in to preparing for my future that I wasn't paying any attention to my last bit of academic work. One day my English professor pulled me aside and shared her concern about my withering grade. I nervously told her I was going to the NBA after the semester and she burst out an "Oooooohhhh, I see," and proceeded to congratulate me and assure me I was okay to focus on basketball.

After a total of eight months on FSU's campus, I packed my things. Ma and Ron picked me up. I'd agreed to head out to Impact basketball in Las Vegas in a week with Jeff for pre-draft training. There I'd stay with Perry, another agent in Jeff's firm, and keep developing. Preparing for the draft became my full-time gig, which was surreal. No more school, family, or real responsibility outside of getting picked as high as I could. It was a ton of work. I experienced my first endorsement opportunities and media training.

My agent's advice was to only work out for three teams to appear more exclusive. First up was Boston. I was about to work out for an NBA basketball team, and they actually wanted to work me out. It wasn't some sketchy back-alley workout that I snuck into. I couldn't believe it. I called Coach Gates as I drove to the gym.

"I'm nervous yo," I remember blurting out into the phone. I laughed to take the edge off.

"You're going to kill it, man," he assured me with confidence.

"You think so Coach?"

"I know so. Take it back to when you had your first workout in front of a college coach. It was me, and you killed it. I mean, you was ugly but you killed it. Knees bigger than your thighs and all."

We busted out laughing. "Coach, you so wrong for that, but I appreciate it." That was Coach Gate's gift, knowing what to say. I had been here before, but this time my knees weren't bigger than my thighs. I finished the drive bumping my jams and assuring myself all I needed to do was get my mind right and my game would take care of the rest.

I was already inside the gym getting warm by the time Danny Ainge and his crew showed up with Jeff. All eyes peered at me while they talked amongst themselves. I shot lightly with the trainer who would take me through the workout.

When it was time for business, the Boston team, and Jeff, sat on the sidelines, poker-faced as the trainer and I started to get into it. Nothing but the sound of the ball and the eerie feeling of surveillance. It took me a few clanks to get comfortable, but I got there. Nerves faded the more parts of the workout I executed and the more I saw lips moving and fingers jotting down notes. It went well overall, better than I expected. When the drills were over,

I took a seat in front of them, gearing up for the questions Jeff told me to expect.

"Do you do drugs?"

"No sir." (Confession: I smoked weed quite a bit my last year of high school and after my FSU season. Pot made me cooler in high school, and in college it took the edge off. But I had laid off weeks before now.)

"What's your mindset at this point in your life?"

"I just want to get better."

"What are you into?"

"Basketball and video games." (That was my life. *Call of Duty* was my game.)

After the handshakes and closing remarks, it was over. I had completed my first workout and had no idea what would happen next. I wouldn't find out until a month later, draft day, June 22.

Back to the grind. I knocked out the remaining two workouts for Philly and Phoenix and headed back to New York to take on draft week.

DRAFT DAY

The week was full of interviews and meetings with reporters and league personnel. The day itself was a chaotic, adrenaline-charged blur. I wondered if any of the other draftees had enough presence of mind to really enjoy the moment. If that was even possible. Most of the guys looked chill and confident, taking in stride what was probably one of the best days of their lives. Time ticked by on fast-forward for me.

It was finally time to answer the question Coach Gates had asked me three years ago. *"Who is going to be at your table in the green room when your name is called?"* Mom, Dad, Coaches Gates and Hamilton, and my agent Jeff, sat with me when Commissioner Adam Silver announced, "With the sixth pick in the 2017 NBA Draft, the Orlando Magic select Jonathan Isaac from Florida State University."

Heads turned toward me. Cheers resounded. Lights flashed. The first hugs went to Mom and Pops, then my former college coaches, and finally my agent. The walk up to the stage where a black Orlando Magic hat was waiting for me, and the handshake and pictures with Commissioner Silver was surreal. My fate was sealed; I made it to the league.

After the haze of interviews and sound bites, me, Coaches Gates, and Jeff's assistant Amanda hit a pizza shop walking distance from the hotel. Low key and chill summed up the night. It was fitting. I didn't quite grasp the weight of what had just happened and what it would mean for my family and my life. I heard other draftees booked private rooms or VIP sections at fancy lounges and clubs.

I remember getting back to my room and just standing in front of the mirror looking at myself. I said, "You did it man! You're in the NBA." But the words came out more shocked than celebratory. Coach CY was right. Why was I so worried and afraid? If I knew this was going to happen, I would have handled everything differently. I wouldn't have stressed about people's thoughts or my own. But it doesn't work like that. At the end of the night though, I knew I couldn't go to sleep without thanking God. Even if I was out here sinning, He was somewhere up in all of this.

I got on my knees. "Thank you, God. That was dope. I made it." Sleep came fast that night.

The next morning, I boarded a private jet to Orlando. Not only was draft day over, but so was life as I had previously known it. My followers on social media soared, my texts were flooded, and basketball had just become my full-time occupation.

HOME SWEET HOME

The transition from college kid to NBA player was abrupt. One day I'm swiping my debit card linked to Ma's account, praying she put money in it so I could eat with my friends. A few weeks later, I'm buying that same woman a brand-new car in cash. I didn't know much about money at the time, but Coach Gates helped me pick a great financial advisor. I felt honored to be in a position where my mother didn't have to work multiple jobs and I could help my siblings when they needed it. But it's a tough responsibility at nineteen. It's not the easiest thing in the world decoding the nuances of when to say yes, when to say no, and when to hang up the phone. When you sign your contract, you're not thinking, and no one is warning you about the importance of making healthy boundaries.

To help newbies like me adjust, however, the NBA has a mandatory Rookie Transition Program. All the new rooks gathered for a few days in New Jersey over the summer before the season. We listened to motivational speakers and attended workshops on topics like character and ethics, personal and social responsibility, and the dangers of alcohol and drug abuse. We heard plenty of horror stories of being at the wrong place at the wrong time. We were warned to watch out for people trying to take advantage, from groupies to anyone with a business card who was interested in us for our money or athletic status. In summation, "Don't do drugs, lay off the booze, and try not to get duped, or your story will be told in the next year's Rookie Transition Program."

I'll never forget a group of us rooks chilling during some free time. We were talking about the caliber of women in our new respective cities and how well each of us were faring so far. When the attention got to Semi Ojeleye, he made a startling confession. "I'm not into that," he said. "I'm a virgin."

The guys in our circle howled with laughter. I'm embarrassed to admit that I laughed along with them. I'm sure all of us were padding our stats to impress the guy next to us. I know I was. The last thing I wanted to do was come off as lame. But I was still stuck on what Semi said.

Above the cacophony of tomfoolery, I turned toward him and asked, "Why?"

"I'm a Christian," he replied.

I respected Semi all the more as soon as the reason left his mouth, thinking back on my youth group desire to be authentic. I wasn't there yet. Frankly, I don't know if my life and headspace ever matched up to that desire. So not proud to say this, but I dove back into the lewd conversation. I was hellbent on experiencing what the NBA life had to offer, on and off the court. The picture in my head of a real man was not wearing a suit and sitting in a church service. I genuinely respected Semi's convictions. But I silently believed a real man had money, women, and prestige. As far as I knew, I was climbing toward the summit. I had no idea that God would show me a much more important mountain to climb.

READY, SET, TRAIN

Training started right away. Me and Wes Iwundu, the other player I'd been drafted with, hit the ground running. We bonded over the rookie experience. Having someone going through the same process with me made it easier, even though I was a couple years younger than him.

I'm not gonna lie. My first couple of workouts were pretty awkward. Lots of stop-and-go from me asking for clarification. I'm sure I looked like a robot, trying my best not to make any mistakes. The moment I'd hear, "Let's take some threes," from above the arch, my stomach would turn, and my palms would get sweaty. Shooting particularly heightened my nerves because of all the chatter heading into the draft about my ability to shoot. Imagine my surprise when after one of the workouts a trainer mentioned, "You're going to be a great shooter in this league." I didn't know if he said it because I shot well or because I didn't. Either way, I accepted the compliment with a nod. Moving forward, my strategy was to keep my head down and to work really hard. That strategy was my go-to answer come Media Day.

Media Day, which started on September 24, marked the unofficial start of the season. By that time, Coach Gates and my agent had helped me settle into a one-bedroom in a high-rise downtown apartment. I went super minimal. A bed, a couch, a TV, a couple of towels, plates, silverware, and my beloved gaming system. That's all I needed in order to manage. I was wary of spending money because growing up we didn't have much to spend.

Think of Media Day as the first day of school. All your classmates are back from camp, staycations, and beach getaways. You reunite with friends you made in the previous grade and see new faces. Rookies, like new students, are looking to integrate and make their mark. Everyone, rooks and vets alike, are trying to feel each other out, see what's up and what's what. Only difference between Media Day and the first of school is on Media Day, every pair of eyes in sports news are on you, trying to predict your potential and the trajectory of the team for the upcoming season.

I woke up on Media Day drenched in sweat. *Just lay low and keep it moving*, I'd need to remind myself constantly. The team met all of our supporting staff that day, from the GM to the team shrink. Media interviews were already lined up, and the reporters were already talking about the first day of training camp, which was still two days away. It seemed like everyone had questions for me. *What were my plans to dominate? Who was I ready to go against? What could fans expect out of me that season*? Meanwhile I had questions of my own: *Are my teammates going to like me? Are they going to accept me? What expectations did the coaches have of me and would I live up to them?* Essentially the same questions I'd been asking my whole life.

I decided to keep a journal through Media Day and training camp. I'd never journaled before. The idea came out of nowhere as I sat on my couch, overthinking what the next days would bring. On the night of Media Day, and the nights of the two days of training camp, I wrote:

> September 24 "Media Day":
>
> Today was tough, a lot of questions about what people should expect from me and it made me

anxious. Made me more aware that the season starts so soon. I feel overwhelmed and kind of like when the ball goes up for tip off it will be the end of my life. There was good stuff about today, too. I had fun with Mel.[6] and she made me feel good about who I am. She told me I'm different from a lot of other guys in the league and it made me feel special. I want to always remain humble and care about the people around me. Soon will be my first training camp. I'm a little nervous and I have every right to be. This is all new to me and should be treated as such. Each and every day is a learning experience for me. Tomorrow, try your best to get comfortable. Learn and put things into perspective.

September 26 "First day of training camp":

Today was up and down for me. I expected myself to be nervous at times and I was but at the same time I did a lot of good things. I picked up on the pick and roll defense quickly and I had a few good plays on 5 and 5. Overall, for the first practice I learned a lot and that is what I set out to do. The second practice was definitely harder for me. I caught myself drifting and not staying in the moment. I also was in my head entirely too much. My job is to learn and I did but still being too critical of myself. After practice I did the magic 105[7] and I struggled, but the truth is I was going to struggle before I even started shooting because I told myself I was. I try too hard to be perfect and then I beat myself up when I'm not. Dave Love[8] said it best, "The day my teammates and the magic organization expect me to be great is not today."

September 28:

Today was a really good day for me! My head was clear, and I was simply competing. I kept telling myself to just be a learner. Be comfortable in where I'm at in my press and just focus on growth. My shot felt pretty good today and it's simply because I am a good shooter. Not great, not bad, simply good. And every day is a building block. There will be good days and bad days but this day was a good day!!

In three days and three journal entries, you can see the rollercoaster that was my mind. I tried to be perfect in fear of not being perfect, and roundabout I went. I struggled to separate my worth from my performance. Trying to be positive and speaking what I wanted to believe pulled me from the depths occasionally. But without the words being rooted in something other than my mouth, they had little long-term success. The pattern of good days, bad days, and terrible days continued as the team prepared for game one.

GAME TIME

Just so you know, no one briefed me on what a game day in the NBA was going to look like. No timeline, no breakdown, nothing. Prior to tip off, during the pregame shooting on court, I tried to keep my mind occupied. I listened to music, stretched, and ate. I made one mistake. I put on my warmups because it was cold and made a mental note to put my jersey on before heading out for the game. Next thing I knew, Coach Vogel walked in for his pregame speech. When he finished, we huddled up and headed out, all wearing warmups. I didn't think anything of it. We all looked the same, and I just followed everyone out. Of course, I was the only one who wasn't wearing his jersey under the jacket.

Finally, at almost the end of the first quarter, my teammate Bismack Biyombo, handed me my jersey just before I was about to check in and enter the game. But not without getting the whole exchange on video from behind the bench. Everyone and even me got a laugh out of it. Welcome to the league, rook!

I played nearly twenty minutes that night, taking home four points, eight rebounds and two blocks. Overall, it wasn't too bad on the mental. I was nervous for sure but just focused on playing really hard.

For the next month, my schedule was the same. Wake up, go to practice, play a game, play PS4, get into some extra curriculars with Wes, and chill out. I was still real insecure around my teammates, in the game, and even in the city for that matter. It made me uncomfortable to be the center of attention as people walked up for pictures and autographs. I played hard defense, and left offense alone. When my friends, family, or media would ask about my usual offensive aggressiveness not being there, I'd say I needed time to get comfortable. But at this pace, I'd need all the time in the world. I tried to cope using things that would take my mind off the game. Hours and hours of Fortnite and the thrill of intoxication and nightlife. How much better could life get?

DUSTING OFF THE BIBLE

Did I want to go to chapel? Seven words that would change the trajectory of my spiritual life, and with it, every aspect of life itself. When my teammate Elfrid Payton asked me that question, I had no idea what he meant. He explained that an hour before every game, a Christian chapel service is held open to both teams. I agreed, thinking to myself that I could use a good word. But I was not prepared in the slightest for what came out of the chaplain's mouth.

He began with a brief summary of what we could expect. "Here in chapel we'll take a topic, idea, or verse and do our best to tackle it in the short time we have together. The verse I have for you guys tonight is a simple one, but if you let it, it can change everything." The chaplain then read from Luke 6:46: "But why do you call

Me 'Lord, Lord,' and not do the things which I say? You see guys, the true test of our faith is not who we claim to be, but who we are in action."

Drop the mic.

My first thought was that I'd never heard that verse before, and the second was that it had me written all over it. He continued his sermon which went something like this:

"Jesus goes on to say that those who come to Him and hear his words and don't carry them out are foolish. Their houses, no matter how pleasing to the eye or architecturally sound, are ultimately built on hollow ground and truthless claims. When hardship and the battles of life we all face come, our structures built with our hands and feeble knowledge will prove insufficient. And the destruction on that day will be great. But in the same breath, Jesus promises that if you and me take Him at His word and put them into practice, we're counted as wise. For making the free decision to build on what is solid and unchanging. True and loving. Able to withstand the mightiest storm."

I was in awe because I knew every word of it was true.

I never knew Jesus to be so confrontational, not until His words were confronting me. Guilty as charged. I'd be the first one to pray after a bad game or throw on some gospel music to feel better about my prior decisions, but I was not at all focused on what pleased God or what He asked of me

This message stayed on my mind from those fifteen minutes, to during the game that night, to practice the next day. It never left. I was perplexed about the possible realness of God beyond the childhood stories, family traditions, saying I'm a Christian because it sounds good or mumbling a prayer in a youth group service years ago. I started to imagine what it would really mean for it to all be true. What my life would look like if I actually believed. I was at a crossroad between thoughts in my mind and what I felt in my heart. I couldn't just go on with my life like that day never happened.

The song and dance of lukewarm allegiance to something I hadn't fully understood ended as soon as that chaplain opened his mouth. I decided I was either in or not. And there was only one way to find out.

I did what every reasonable person would. I set out on a one-man odyssey to explore the reality of Christianity beyond what I already knew. I began with researching Christian apologetics, a term I learned while looking up why people thought Christianity was true. It means the defense for the Christian faith. C.S. Lewis, Frank Turek, John Lennox, William Lane Craig, and N.T. Wright, are just a few of the extremely learned, devout men we call apologists. I'd stay up late watching videos on so many different topics from the reliability of the New Testament manuscripts to the Kalam Cosmological Argument. It states that whatever begins to exist has a cause of its existence. The universe began to exist, and therefore, the universe has a cause to its existence. I even signed up for an online apologetics course with Biola University to further explore the existence of God. I started to talk about the possible realness of Jesus with a friend named Kevin, who was a couple years older than me and worked for the team in player development. We agreed to go to church and did so whenever we were in town.

I was multitasking the season with my spiritual investigation when one of them got sidetracked. On November 11, over a month into the season, we laced 'em up against the Denver Nuggets. As I swatted a shot from Emmanuel Mudiay, I landed on his foot. As my ankle turned, I heard a pop. I left the arena that night in a walking boot with a grade-three ankle sprain. I'd miss seventeen consecutive games and wouldn't return to play until December, when I would only play two games before getting hurt again the same way, only to miss another twenty-seven games.

League injuries are common, but I never expected two of that magnitude so early in my rookie year. I also never expected what would happen in my life once I was on the sidelines. That injury opened the door for me to become who I am today.

CHAPTER 6

ON THE COURT, OFF THE COURT

WHEN IT CAME TO MY FAITH AWAKENING, God didn't inundate me with all knowledge and revelation at once. It was more like morsels of truth that appeared in ordinary moments, through divine connections, conversations, and collisions that I didn't orchestrate. One of the most important revelations was realizing that everything was connected. That the same me playing basketball was the same me playing video games and hanging out at the clubs. I was me wherever I was and whatever I chose to do.

It was fine until I realized it wasn't.

DIVINE COLLISIONS

I met the man who would champion my faith investigation—and challenge the part of me that was getting in the way—while I was injured, in the beginning of my rookie year. One day as I waited for the elevator in the lobby of my apartment, a man with a thick Bahamian accent stopped me and said, "I know how you can be great."

Um, okay. I thought it was an odd thing to say. I could tell he didn't know who I was just by his remark.

"Tell me."

Without missing beat, he continued, "You have to know Jesus."

I groaned on the inside. *Was this really happening*? It felt like when you've just let your guard down with someone and then they immediately try to sell you something. Like a multivitamin or an essential oil that has changed their life. If it was Jesus this guy was selling, thankfully I could stop him right there.

"Yeah, I'm a Christian, so..." my voice trailed off hoping that's all he needed to hear. *Keep it moving, buddy*. The guy kept talking. He introduced himself as Doc, and he lived in the building. We parted ways after the short elevator ride, and I didn't give our fleeting conversation a second thought.

But I started seeing him more and more. We passed each other in the parking garage, in the lobby. "Let me take you to lunch," he'd offer, but I'd dodge the question by mumbling an excuse.

What does he want from me? I'd think to myself. My defenses would get higher each time we'd pass, out of fear of being taken advantage of. Yet, running into him so often made me wonder. The next unplanned rendezvous finally prompted me to tell him, “If I see you again, I’ll go to lunch with you.”

I did, and off we went. Doc and I casually chatted about basketball. By then he knew what I did for a living, though I didn’t know what he did. As we talked about God, I remember chewing on my sandwich and telling him, “I don’t like pastors. They’re hypocrites who just want your money.” This, of course, coming from the same person who declared he was a Christian. Doc didn’t say much in response. We continued sharing where we each were from and got to know a bit about each other. And that was that. Minutes after I left the restaurant, I tapped on his contact in my phone and swiped left. Didn’t see him around for a while.

Still nursing my injury and having time off from playing, my friend from player development and I dug into reading the Bible. Thanksgiving was a week away, and one afternoon, we read Matthew 25:40, which says, “Whatever you did for one of the least of these brothers and sisters of mine, you did for me” (NIV). I had an idea.

“Burgers!” I blurted out that afternoon. “Let’s buy a bunch of burgers at Mickey D’s and pass them out to the homeless on Thanksgiving!” He was all in, though neither one of us was quite sure how or where to start.

That night Akii, my old trainer who I still stayed in touch with, and his wife popped up in town to hang out.

We decided to watch a Christian flick. I hate saying it, but the film was so cheesy that halfway through, the three of us bolted and slipped into the theatre playing *Thor*. Afterwards, we sat outside under the night sky for an hour talking basketball and how my rehab was going.

Akii, who was always invested in my spirituality, casually asked my thoughts as it pertained to God. I didn't blow him off like I used to. I admitted I was actively seeking truth through reading and watching videos on Christian apologetics. "I'm searching for God to make Himself real to me," I said. When we parted ways, Akii assured me that if I genuinely sought after God, it would only be a matter of time until I found Him.

As I drove out of the parking lot of the downtown theater, a familiar car was pulling in. The driver and I rolled down our windows at the same time. As soon as I saw it was Doc, I had to laugh. Akii's words rang in my head. I thought, *God must want this guy in my life.*

Before Doc had a chance to spit out, "What's up, man?" I shot out the first words. "You and me. Breakfast tomorrow."

I drove home thinking if I had stayed and watched the rest of the first film or spoke with Akii any longer or shorter, I wouldn't have run into Doc. *There's no way this is just a coincidence.*

The next morning as Doc and I chewed syrup-drenched pancakes, I told him about my plan to feed the homeless. Yeah, I was definitely trying to show off.

"Burgers, huh? Like fast food?" he asked, hiking up an eyebrow.

"Yeah, like you know how the Bible in Matthew 25:40 tells us about the least of these?"

"Jonathan, you can't do it like that. If you're going to feed people, you have to do it right. Look, I have a catering company. If you buy the food, I'll have my people cook it and help you serve it."

"I'm down with that," I said, nodding. It was the start of something new.

GOING ALL IN

We left breakfast and I followed him to Sam's Club. On the way I remember thinking, *What in the world are you doing, Jonathan? You don't even know who this guy really is!* I answered my own question by telling myself it all felt right, so I followed. I spent seven hundred bucks, which was actually a lot for my frugal self to fork over. We loaded the food into a van Doc had arranged to meet us there. We shook hands, and he was gone. I thought, *Well, Jonathan, you just fed this man's family for a year!*

A couple days later I got a text from Doc with an address and a time. Me and Kevin pulled up that day in disbelief as we saw a line of maybe two hundred people that snaked around one corner of a strip mall. As we walked around the back of the building, I spotted Doc and he greeted me with excitement. There were tables nicely set up outside decked with thanksgiving favorites and a crew of people managing the whole thing. I put on a hairnet and jumped in line serving people that were obviously in need. I asked the pretty young lady next to me how in the world all this got here. She said Doc told them about what I had wanted to do, how they had passed out flyers on the streets for days, and how she appreciated my heart. Her name was Takita. She would become my wife, but there's much more to the story.

We served about two hundred and fifty people. It felt humbling to be part of something I knew was a blessing to the community. I was really moved by their faces, filled with gratitude and awe that I was who I was, doing what I was doing. I'd never done something like that before. As we wrapped up the feeding festivities, Doc pulled me aside. "Would you be open to having me and some other people pray over your injured ankle?"

"Sure, that's fine," I replied. I couldn't remember the last time someone prayed for me in front of me. Takita, Doc, his wife, and a few others took me inside of what appeared to be a church in the plaza. Doc's wife poured oil over my puffy ankle as Doc knelt at my feet and prayed. It was awkward, for me at least, towering above a handful of people I had just met as they prayed for me. I noted the sincerity with which Doc asked God for my healing as the others agreed with strong "Amens." Awkward feels aside, I felt the love.

I drove home that night thinking about how perfectly the feeding unfolded. It must have been orchestrated by God. And to think, it only happened from reading a Bible verse and telling a man I knew almost nothing about that I wanted to pass out burgers to the homeless. And even that only came about because I accepted someone's invitation to a chapel service. I felt accounted for, like someone was interested in my well-being by influencing my direction. It was God, of course. He had to care about me.

That night, alone in my apartment, I knelt beside my bed for the first time since moving in. As tears spilled from my eyes, I whispered, "Jesus, you are real." I remembered some lines from a prayer I was told to recite at a youth group service many years ago. "I repent of my sins. Come into my heart. Be Lord of my life."

Doc had invited me to church the following day. I remember telling him, "If you're cool, your pastor's got to be cool." Imagine my surprise when he appeared behind the podium after being introduced as the pastor of the church. In hindsight, I was glad Doc—who was now officially Bishop Dr. Durone Hepburn—didn't tell me he was a pastor the first time we met. If he had, no multiple run-ins would have budged my self-righteous judgment, and our introduction would have gone no further.

Hearing Doc preach was awesome. I didn't know all of that fervor could fit in such a small man. He was passionate and meaningful, like he took very seriously the weight of his position. I remember him preaching about faith that Sunday. He said that faith is the commodity of heaven like money is the commodity of earth. You get the world's attention with money but capture God's attention with faith. When you spend money, it's gone, but when you move in faith, out of belief in God, the ripples last for eternity. I didn't see it then, but I moved in faith when I followed Doc to Sam's. Think about it, and now here I was, glued to a seat in church as he preached. He was funny, charismatic, and frank all at the same time. From then on I was a member of J.U.M.P. Ministries Global Church.

Over the next month I'd attend services and hang out with Doc every now and then in my free time. I deleted phone numbers, unfollowed people on social media, and stopped going to the clubs. Hearing him preach more and more about the mind and the heart and how Jesus had to be first in our lives was like water on a hot day. "I never thought about it like that" is something I'd say to myself during every sermon. I'd find myself thinking about the different topics he'd preach on as I was on the sideline during practices and games still recovering. If I didn't have Doc or the church, I'm not sure where I would've been mentally, having to sit out.

As our friendship grew, Doc asked me to accompany him to 5:30 a.m. prayer at the church. I had never woken up for anything that early since preseason conditioning at FSU.

I showed up with my hair a mess and breath hot. Doc explained that prayer was simply a conversation with God. I could be honest and tell Him anything. Worship, repent, ask, pray for someone else—all of that, Doc offered, was prayer. He placed a blanket on the ground in front of the altar for me to lay on. I thought it was weird having never prayed on the floor in front of lit candles as worship music played, but I followed the flow. Five minutes in, I was asleep. When I woke up, I noticed that Takita was a few yards away on her own blanket. An hour had already gone by.

Sensing my frustration, Doc assured me that my prayer life would grow as I worked at it. He was right. I continued to show up for prayer and saw progress in small increments, from five minutes to fifteen and so on.

I was in such a good place I almost forgot about my real job being basketball. I had healed up and was ready to get back on the court. I stumbled through my first game back, even though I proclaimed that God had me. My stomach still ached when I saw the huge crowd. We fought hard, but we lost to Detroit. I expected to feel different out there after going to church for a while, but the same thoughts of insecurity and feelings of anxiety surfaced.

Three days later, a day or two before Christmas, facing the Bulls in Chicago, I reinjured the same ankle in only my second game back. We also lost, again. Since injuring my ankle the first time on November 11, I'd only played for a total of thirty-six minutes in two games. After the game in Chicago, I was going to be off the court for the next two months.

On the flight back to Orlando, I remember looking out the window with tears rolling down my cheeks. I remained locked in that position the whole time so none of my teammates would notice my emotional state. I felt the God who revealed himself to me was off somewhere else, focusing his attention on someone else.

Discouraged and alone, I trudged home through a sleeping building to an empty apartment.

FEELING THE LOVE

It was two o'clock in the morning when I pushed open my front door. Expecting darkness, my balance wobbled as I was suddenly bathed in sparkling light. Before me, I saw a white Christmas tree cradling strings of blue bulbs. It wasn't there when I left. It stood around six feet tall, glowing in the colors of my team.

The fog of the early morning and the battering disappointment I felt withdrew into a warmth in my gut. The blinding tree had to have been Doc and his wife. He had come over before I left, and seeing how messy my place was, he offered to have it cleaned while I was gone. I had given permission for the security guard at the front desk to let him in. Doc and his wife were like guardian angels. They'd often check up on me and bring me food. But this was different. They'd created magic in my bland space.

It took a few minutes before I realized there were gifts under the tree. I'd later learn that Doc's wife had told some of the elders and leaders of the church what she and Doc were doing, and they offered to pitch in and buy me gifts. I can't imagine trying to figure out what to get an NBA player they barely knew. I appreciated the fact that they even wanted to try.

I went to bed that night without a thought of my reinjured ankle. Instead, I saw a picture of the God who had not forgotten me but had revealed Himself to me through human hands and hearts. Though I was a relative stranger in a new place, God was giving me what I needed and didn't have.

We often think of love as a feeling, but my understanding of love began to change. One of the times I sat in service thinking, *I never thought about it like that,* was when Bishop taught, "Love is not what you say. Love is what you do. It's an action word." I remember him beginning to quote John 3:16: "For God so loved the world that he...." And he stopped, giving the congregation the opportunity to answer.

"Gave," they shouted.

"Yes," Doc continued and finishing the thought, "And God gave His best." The love I felt from Doc, his wife, and the church was doing something for me I couldn't identify just yet. But I knew I was beginning to trust my new friend more.

I'll never forget the day Doc knocked on my door holding a large bowl, a kettle, and a box of Epsom salt. "We're going to soak your ankle," he told me with a grin.

"What? No! You don't have to do that man," I protested. Eventually, I let him in.

I'll admit, I wasn't used to attention and love like this. So much so that I was eerie of its genuineness. It wasn't just this one-time deal of kindness and generosity. It was ongoing. If I was home during mealtime, Doc's wife would always make extra and bring me up a helping of whatever she had cooked. Uber Eats was in my favorites in my phone, so a home-cooked meal was like finding a handwritten thank you card in a heap of bills and local advertisements. I can't tell you how many times since that trip away to Chicago I came home to a clean apartment. Doc's wife and the church had even stocked my pad a few times with essentials like paper towels and groceries. Doc, his wife, and the church were meeting my needs without being asked to.

These people saw my aloneness, my hunger for community, and my desire for God. And they fed me, in almost every sense of the word. But no one, not even Doc, knew the struggles of fear and insecurity inside me. To external eyes, I was just a young and charming high-draft pick NBA player on hiatus until healthy.

Doc was the first one to catch a glimpse. God made sure Doc was at the right place at the right time.

A LIFE LESSON

I remember sitting in my car in the parking deck of my building around midnight. I was back in the lineup that night after missing the last twenty games. I switched off the engine and cut the lights. One tear slowly trickled down my cheek. As the weight of my thoughts increased, so did my tears. I replayed the scene of an airball. A blown layup. A rookie mistake. The berating self-diatribe kicked in.

This is how you make your debut?

What's wrong with you?

What were you even doing out there?

A knock on my passenger side window interrupted the internal drama. It was Doc coming home from Friday night Bible study.

"Can I come in?" he asked softly as I rolled down the window.

I bobbed my head.

Doc walked around the car and slipped into the passenger seat. "How was the game?"

He obviously knew it didn't go well, so I chose not to answer that question. "I'm letting everyone down," I said instead.

"Who is everyone?"

"Just everyone that's expecting me to play great."

"You being great is a process, Jonathan. You know that, right? It's okay if you weren't at your best tonight. You have more games. You're going to come back better. See it from that perspective." Doc's words sailed with a gentle ease through his thick accent.

I was disarmed, turning my head toward the neat rows of parked cars.

Then Doc said something, which would stick with me forever. "Jonathan, I want you to always remember this: off the court, on the court. As it is in life, so is it in basketball."

I wrinkled my forehead.

"You can't hide from you, Jonathan," Doc began to explain. "Basketball isn't your problem; you are your problem. You take you into every area of your life. It's about how you think and feel about you in your heart. What you believe about who you are as a person, as a man. When you face your fears, anxieties, and insecurities, your God-given gift of basketball will line up. You need to ground yourself in the unchanging truth of God's word. You've allowed lies and the perception of others to shape how you see yourself. You must find your identity in the One who paid for it."

Wiping my tears I asked, "How do I do that?"

"Continue to put God first. Focus on developing your relationship with Him and you'll grow to trust who He is and who He says you are. Make everything about Him and not you. Come out of the driver's seat and let Him lead the way. Let what He says and how He sees you in His Word become your truth."

Doc was the first person to bring to my attention my problem. I wasn't embarrassed or ashamed by his assessment; I understood his point. *On the court, off the court.* I needed to deal with me, first, not my jump shot.

My whole life I tried to be something more than me, to gain attention, approval, and acceptance. Rejection told me I wasn't enough, so basketball was my ticket to receiving everything I ever wanted. But I could never become who I was made to be if my mind and heart were clouded with fear and insecurity. If I could combat my fears and self-doubt with the truth of God's word, I could be free. Not only in basketball, but in life. I was ready to work on this inner change. Turns out, so was God.

AN UNEXPECTED OPPORTUNITY

I remember lying in bed one night; I was tired but couldn't sleep. My mind was stuck on what I had read in James 1:22-25.

> "But be doers of the word, and not hearers only, deceiving yourselves. For if anyone is a hearer of the word and not a doer, he is like a man observing his natural face in a mirror; for he observes himself, goes away, and immediately forgets what kind of man he was. But he who looks into the perfect law of liberty and continues in it, and is not a forgetful hearer but a doer of the work, this one will be blessed in what he does."

I thought to myself, *If we are doers of God's Word, it follows that He would have to bless us.* This scripture is a promise based on the condition of obedience. I kid you not, I started sweating as I laid there. A rush of adrenaline swept over me. I heard the words in my mind, "Preach." This directive wasn't audible but it might just as well have been. My response was practically automatic, which surprised me. I got up out of bed and started to speak out loud what I was thinking in front of my mirror. As I kept on "preaching," the internal voice rose in volume. "Preach!!" I began to raise my voice, uttering a sermon I had never prepared, outlined, or even thought about to an audience of one.

> "We are so focused on what we want from God that we skip over what He wants from us. When we are obedient because we believe, it gets God's attention, and causes Him to move on our behalf. Matthew 6:33 says if we would seek first the kingdom of heaven and His righteousness, only then would the things we need be added unto us."

I carried on in front of the mirror about how our responsibility is to strive for obedience (as hard as it is) and not perfection, and how the responsibility of blessings, provisions, and protection rests with the only One who is capable of providing them. I may have ad-libbed a few "hallelujahs" and "Can I get an amens?" but that was the gist of my imaginary preaching. And I didn't even have to leave my bedroom. Pretty wild. I had never before experienced anything like that.

I woke up the next morning asking myself if I was crazy. *What was that last night? Did I manufacture what happened*? I couldn't have. I mean, think about it. The last thing I would ever even want to do is preach. I was terrified of public speaking. I remembered nearly passing out from having to speak to a bunch of kids while I was at Florida State.

A few days later, I told Doc what happened.

Without hesitation he replied, "That was the Holy Spirit nudging you. I think you should share on a Sunday! I'm watching you grow and develop, and the more I think about it, that was revelation God was downloading in your spirit."

Bring what, where, on a what now?

Before I could even respond, he continued. "Also, I think you should invite your teammates."

"Absolutely not!" I said, laughing. "You can't be serious."

"You are going to do great," my mentor reassured me. "People would love to hear from you. A voice different from mine. And Jonathan, you know the Word. Just share what God has given you.

"No way man." "Is it normal for you to just ask people to preach out of the blue?"

"Not typically," Bishop admitted. "But you're not normal

and I feel this is something God is calling you to do. Give me your decision only after you really pray about it."

I was terrified—and then some. I'd never been this kind of scared before. Not even on the court. Trying to do faith in a real way was new territory for me, unlike playing ball most of my life. Some of the people I would be preaching to have been Christians longer that I've been alive, and I'm supposed to lecture them about obedience? I could already imagine what they'd be thinking—*who in the world does this rich NBA player think he is*? Once I'd flop behind the pulpit, I'd probably have to find another church.

As days passed, any time I thought about the possibility of going through with preaching, my heart rate would rise. I pondered all the reasons this was a terrible idea. The look that would be on my teammates' faces. Up until this point, they only knew the Jonathan that liked Hennessy and Coke, not the one that had been growing in faith behind the scenes. Now I'm supposed to tell them to come hear me preach? Everything that was me said, "No."

I was faithful to Doc's instructions, even though I knew if I prayed about it the answer would be yes. As I lay at the altar one morning, my mind shifted back to following behind Doc on the way to Sam's Club, and then to our cars perfectly aligning on my way home from the movie theater, then to me on my knees beside my bed the night after we fed the homeless. As terrified as I was, I knew God was up to something. I knew I wasn't here, at this moment in my life, because I just wanted to be here. I knew I was being led. The ball was in my court. Preach, yes or no. Faith as I had been taught it or fear as I had lived it. It was my choice.

I got up from the altar and called Doc. I told him I'd do it.

I approached my teammates one by one and told them I'd be preaching my first sermon the upcoming Sunday. The response was okay. Nobody laughed. With each ask, the pressure lessened.

Now the hard part.

A STEP FORWARD IN FAITH

I stood at that podium with Doc sitting behind me. I preached in public for the first time. I shared about the wackiness of how the heck I got there in the first place by meeting Doc. How, when I made it to the league, I thought to myself that I had won life, and in a short time, I found that life had so much more to offer. And that for the first time, being planted in a church and committed to Jesus, I felt like I finally knew where my feet were. Not that I had arrived yet in full understanding or belief in Christ, but that my whole life I had lived in a fog of my own thoughts, being pushed along by talent. And now I've experienced a taste of freedom, and I'm sold.

The meat of my sermon was on obedience. I shared with the church I had grown to love that the same way as a boy

I expected my parents to come through with what they promised me if I did what they asked, is the same way we can expect from our heavenly father when we strive to live by faith in the confinements of His Word. Bishop always says, "We don't give to get, but we expect." It's not magic nor is God a genie, but He has made us promises. Our focus is being obedient to what He asks of us in His Word, and we let Him in His perfect timing take care of the rest.

I concluded to a round of applause. Not because of how well I did, in my opinion, but because this twenty-one-year-old was willing to get up and share despite the mountain of reasons not to. It was respect. Out of all the encouraging comments I received, the one I remembered most came from Takita. I nervously stared into her eyes as she detailed specific things I had said and how she identified with them. She convinced me that my words had made a difference.

I didn't say yes to getting on that stage for or because of me. I didn't muster up the nerve to look my teammates in the face and say I was going to be preaching because I knew I was going to tear the house down. None of them came, by the way. I chose courage in the midst of fear because I believed that God was with me. And His leading and the love and support of people I knew who cared about me was all I needed.

One thing that stayed in my mind even after speaking was how much Doc believed in me the whole time. He saw me on the platform long before I took the stage. As he explained it, his belief was not in me but the God in me.

All in all, I took a step forward with trusting God like Doc promised. I think that's all God wants from us—to trust and obey. To grow in our belief that there's a purpose to His plans and to choose to follow them no matter the fear or obstacle in our way.

As Doc's mantra went, "As it is in life, so is it on the court." Faith was beginning to make appearances in the different areas of my life. Little by little.

CHAPTER 7

LITTLE BY LITTLE

STEPPING OFF THE PULPIT, I felt encouraged about the leap of faith I had taken. I had no idea what would come next or how to juggle the court, my teammates, and my new-found identity in Christ, but I sure was going to find out.

MISINFORMED AND MISUNDERSTOOD

Late in the evening of the day I preached, my phone rang. It was one of my teammates. He told me word had spread about my sermon, and my teammates felt I had thrown them under the bus for not showing up. I was shocked. Unbeknownst to me, the media had already watched my sermon, which uploaded to YouTube after I spoke, and ran with the following narrative: "Jonathan Isaac invited his teammates to hear him preach and none of them showed up." Still on the line, my eyes swelled as I scrolled through Twitter and saw sarcastic memes and comments about how sorry people felt for me.

I assured my teammate my intentions weren't to diss them. I had only mentioned their absence as an obvious observation after sharing with the congregation how difficult it was for me to ask them to come in the first place. This was just the media seizing the opportunity for a story, I pleaded. As soon as I hung up the phone, the tears spilled. My head dropped. *I really messed up. I destroyed the opportunity God gave me. How can I possibly go to practice tomorrow?*

I had Doc on the phone a minute later. As I shared how I completely blew it by mentioning that my teammates didn't show, he interjected, "You don't have anything to be ashamed or upset about, Jonathan." Laughing, he said, "If everybody celebrated you and there wasn't opposition from you speaking, then we should be worried. Be encouraged. You spoke with more courage than I've ever seen from a 22-year-old. It took great boldness to stand behind that pulpit on a Sunday having never preached before. That boldness is on the inside of you. You gave people confidence to face the fears in their own lives. That's life changing!" He further explained to never let the bad take away from the good and that, in time, lies will fade, but truth will always remain. Doc wrapped up our conversation by saying, "Keep it moving, my friend; the darkest hour is always before dawn. If any of your teammates talk to you about this, just be honest. Take this as a learning experience. People will always want a story." I felt better going to bed that night but was still wary of practice the following morning.

Strolling into the locker room with a churning stomach, I was met with a new nickname from one of the guys—"Baby Jesus"! That was a first! I joined in on the few chuckles as I made my way to my chair. Pulling on my warmups, I thought, *Well, Jesus ain't bad company.*

Once we got to the court, Coach Vogel, who was probably briefed on the situation, told us to huddle up. Then he addressed it up front. He said he had seen the video himself and that he wanted everyone to know that from his perspective my intentions were clearly not what was being portrayed in the media.

"Do you have anything to add, Jonathan?" he asked.

"Look, guys," I said, avoiding eye contact. "I'm sorry for the misunderstanding. It's absolutely not what I intended. I'd just like to put this whole thing behind us." Blank stares followed.

Practice was more awkward than usual, like there was a herd of alpacas grazing center court. I was in my head the whole time, worrying about what the guys were thinking and what it would mean for our relationships going forward. Didn't look promising.

For the rest of the season, I was even more detached from the team than before. Thanks in part to minimal verbal communication with my teammates and continued issues with my ankle keeping me out of the lineup. But also because I was at odds with myself. Like most human beings, I craved a sense of belonging. I wanted to feel included and be liked by my teammates. But at the same time, I wanted to do right by God. Some topics and conversations made me uncomfortable, yet wanting to belong tempted me to join in the laughter.

One thing was clear. I couldn't continue to grow in my relationship with God and stay the old Jonathan around my teammates in an attempt to make them comfortable with me and feed my desire to feel accepted.

This truth came alive when I chose to honor God over a deeply held NBA tradition. I had made some major life changes up to this point, but this would test my convictions. I wouldn't be standing behind a pulpit, but I'd be standing all the same.

FACE TO FACE

No rookie comes into the league looking forward to being the team's "do boy." Older guys on every team carry different expectations of their rookies. *Run errands. Keep the locker room clean. Carry the bags. Be a good sport while we're embarrassing you.* This tradition plays back to the very dawn of sports, though today's NBA vets are much nicer to the young players than years back. Sacramento King's Chris Webber made newbie Jason Williams ride under the bus with the luggage from the airport to the team hotel.[9] Something tells me Chris had it pretty bad when he was a rookie. I've heard a story of vets stealing a young teammate's clothes, forcing him to leave the arena in just a towel. In another, a car was destroyed after the experienced players filled a rookie's car with buttered popcorn. Makes me glad I came to the league when I did. Our burden was pretty modest. We rookies had to dance and sing in front of the team or grab food for everyone before the plane ride to the next away game. Pretty tame stuff.

My job was fetching condoms for one of the guys on the team. At the beginning of the season, I considered the task painless, and none of my business. I'd get a text when we touched down in a new city or the night after a game on the road. Then I'd shuffle, sometimes half asleep, to the nearest corner store, make the purchase, shuffle back to the hotel, and slide the stuff under his hotel door. Mission accomplished. No internal conflict about whether what I was doing was right. It was just a duty. A way to keep the peace and earn good rookie points.

After a few more errand runs post-preaching, it wasn't as easy as it used to be. Whenever a text would come through, I'd break out in a sweat. I wasn't comfortable doing it anymore, but I didn't know how to refuse. They didn't cover how to say no to a vet in the Rookie Transition Program.

So I did what I was becoming accustomed to when I had questions. I talked to Doc and spilled the beans on the operation.

"What do you want to do?" he asked. This would become a pattern. I'd figure out later that he'd always ask that question so whatever I decided, it was always my decision.

"I don't want to do it anymore."

"So then, talk to him about it. One on one, man to man."

"What in the world am I supposed to say?" I was scared to death just thinking about it. It was much more comfortable to lay low and blend into the background as I rehabbed and grew as a Christian. To follow Doc's advice meant bringing Jesus with me to the arena. It was one thing to preach about God at church but another thing to do it in the face of someone I was intimidated by. Would he mock me? Laugh? Blab our private convo to the rest of the guys?

Finally, I mumbled, "Okay."

In his wisdom, Doc assured me, "You don't have anything to be afraid of. The Holy Spirit is your strength. You can lean on Him. Always remember that your teammates don't have what you need, you have what they need. Moments of courage like this will save your teammates' lives. One more thing—remember, the Bible says that one person plants a seed, another waters the seed, and God brings the seed to harvest.[10] Meaning it's not your job to save anyone. Just plant the seed and let God do the rest."

I went to bed that night repeating, "One plants, another waters, but God brings the increase."

We were two games into a three-game road trip with a day off before the last one. I was barely in the line, still not being 100 percent. At the hotel that night, I stared at the phone in my hand until my vision blurred. I knew I had to say something before I got the ask.

My heart rate quickened, thumping in my ears like a bass guitar. I remembered Doc's words: "God is going to use moments like these to save your teammates' lives." Trusting in those words, I forced my fingers to type.

Me: "Yo! You mind if I came to your room real quick?" When the three dots appeared on the screen, I held my breath.

"Yea bro."

I knocked on my teammate's door minutes later and made my way to the couch in his hotel room.

"So listen," I began. Suddenly, all of the rehearsed conversation I had diligently prepared disappeared. Instead, I spoke off the cuff, from the heart. "I have nothing but respect for you, and I'm not here to judge you. I've been really trying to do right by God lately in my own life and because of that, uh, I don't feel comfortable getting condoms for you anymore."

Boom, it was out! I wanted to let out a big sigh of relief after being so worked up to say a couple sentences, but I couldn't until I heard his response. Seconds felt like hours.

Finally, he laughed and said, "You good bro! Don't sweat it!"

I left him with this. "I know it's not easy. The last thing I want is for you to feel that I think I am better than you, because I don't and I'm not." I meant every word.

Walking back to my room, I was sobered. I had already been learning from hearing Doc preach that the mere fact that I was trying to change my life showed that my seat wasn't high enough to look down on anyone. Having all the money, women, and fame in the world at your fingertips and no accountability isn't as luxurious as you might think. I know, not only from chasing those things but experiencing them, that like an addict chasing a high, the end is never satisfied. The only difference between me and my teammate was that I was realizing God was never trying to take anything from me. He was actually trying to get something to me. Real inner satisfaction.

I got back to my room and called Doc to let him know how the conversation went. He told me he was so proud of me. Not just for taking steps to walk out Jesus being first outside of the arena, but inside it as well.

I was learning to stand. As Doc phrased it, I was giving God something to work with. Of all the things I could choose to be negative about, from my malfunctioning ankle to my "Baby Jesus" nickname, this convo was one to celebrate. That night, Doc and I prayed that God would draw my teammate more to Him and that he would discover that what he was really chasing was only found in Christ.

I played in just twenty-seven out of eighty-two games my entire rookie season, which meant I was on the court only 32 percent of the time. As the last quarter of the season progressed, the team decided to have me sit out of games and just focus on rehab.

My first year in the league wasn't at all what I thought it would be. But I wasn't mad about it. Sure, it seemed like my ankle stole the show from the court, but in reality if I had never gotten hurt, I wouldn't be on my way to who I was becoming. Maybe God was orchestrating a grand plan from the beginning; I had no qualms with that. I took on the summer, learning more and more about what it meant to really let Him lead. (Jesus, take the wheel.)

Finally, I healed up and was ready for season two.

LEARNING GOD'S LOVE

Season two launched with pretty much an entirely different organization. Trainers, chef, strength coach—all new. In a way, it was kind of my first Media Day all over again. But this time, I was better prepared. I tackled it by telling myself that God had me and that it would be a better Media Day than the last. It was. I wasn't the only one who noticed. The *Orlando Magic Daily* tweeted this about my second Media Day:

> "One media day observation that stuck with me... Jonathan Isaac seemed so at ease and comfortable with himself. Just a different vibe about him. Don't know what that means, but he isn't a rookie anymore."[11]

The change didn't happen because I miraculously started believing in myself. I didn't read a best-selling self-help book. And I didn't wish on a star. Learning to see myself the way God saw me and having others around me who constantly reminded me of what they saw in me and how the best was yet to come did the trick. It all stemmed from one simple principle: unconditional love.

It's amazing what a little love can do. Love that stays steady whether it's a swish or an airball. Unconditional love. God's love. The love I learned about and experienced in my first season playing ball but would only become clear in season two.

We played Boston in our fourth game on October 22, 2018. I didn't hide in the background in what was, at the time, only my thirty-first NBA game. Right out the gate, from the first quarter on, I was free in myself like the Orlando Magic Daily tweeted from Media Day. I wasn't stuck in my head at all. I was playing the game that I loved and having fun doing it. By the time we took home the win 93-90, I had put up eighteen points and twelve rebounds and had hit the game-sealing shot. It felt great being back, healthy in and out.

The headspace of confidence that put me at ease on the court stemmed from the love I was receiving off the court. Trusting I was already loved by God and the people around me unlocked a newfound stability. Kept me grounded where before I'd floundered.

But trouble lurked beneath the surface of a great game so early in the season. Trusting in the love was easy when

I played well and others were singing my praises. Trusting the love in the face of airballs and mediocrity exposed if I was really trusting it at all.

Even though I played well, I silently feared letting down the people who had spent so much time focused on building me up. Fans, the front office, my family, Doc, and my new community. Playing well turned into, "Could I play well again?" And playing bad to me meant I'd lose the love I gained. So, from game to game, I heaped enormous amounts of pressure on myself to live up to what I thought others needed in order to really love me. I wondered if the people who said they loved me would see me as weak or if they would regret their affirmations. Would they give up on me? All these thoughts scrambled as I played.

God began to challenge me with the truth that I was loved unconditionally for me, regardless of my performance. And He used the people around me to do it. Through wins and losses, those around me were fixtures, encouraging me no matter the caliber of my play. Whether it was a good game or a bad one, someone from the church was there to show me they believed in me. They saw greatness in me when I struggled to see it in myself. I got so accustomed to berating myself for every mistake that mistakes were all I saw. I can't tell you how many times I'd come home from a game and find a cake sitting on my kitchen countertop. Sometimes I'd read words in bold, cursive letters like "Man of God" or "You are God's best!" Gleaming in colorful gel icing atop vanilla buttercream frosting. One time the whole church bought tickets and came to a game to show their support. If I chose to plant my identity and worth in my failures, it was completely on me and not because I didn't have someone speaking life into me.

One voice stood out in particular.

Takita and I grew as friends over the summer and through the early season. I admired her love for God but was more intrigued by her nonchalant attitude toward who I was. The Jonathan-Isaac-sixth-pick-in-the-NBA me. She wasn't impressed by which organization signed my paychecks or by my follower count. She was genuinely interested in who I was as an individual and wanted to see that Jonathan grow. It was the same vibe I got from Coach Gates back in the day. She would repeatedly call me great and highlight the positives she saw, no matter the box score.

Unfortunately, I proceeded to accept the love with caution. No matter how genuine were the intentions of the love that surrounded me, I remained suspicious, keeping up the walls around my heart I had built for so long. That was a game I was playing all by myself. It would take some time—and a new laundry room door—for me to fully open my heart and allow myself to be loved.

EXPOSED AND ENCOURAGED

Doc met me at my apartment one night after a game. I'd texted him on the way home. A self-flagellating blurb about my hideous play. While I waited, I moped. Head low, steps heavy. Brooding over the moments when I knew I blew it in front of the packed crowd.

"How was the game?" Doc asked when he showed up.

I snapped back, "Man, you know how the game was!"

"Why are you so upset?" Doc asked. "Be honest, Jonathan."

I sat on the couch, arms crossed, staring at the blank wall. A few minutes of silence passed.

Doc's feet patiently anchored on the hardwood floor, offering the space I needed to share my feelings. Every now and then he'd interrupt the quiet by calling my name. I didn't respond, just sulked deeper into my sadness and anger. Pride kept me from being vulnerable and demanded I refuse to let my friend see me crack.

Doc caught on. With a pat on my back and a shrug of his mouth, he said, "Okay, then. I'm going to leave, Jonathan. You get some sleep."

I was tempted to break character when he turned toward the door, but I didn't say a word. Didn't even nod or turn my head. I was trying to be tough with someone who saw right through me. When the door settled back in its place, the quiet turned up. As did the ensuing war in my mind.

That wasn't cool, man! Are you that afraid of showing weakness? Since when did being honest about how you feel become weak? Why are you like this?

The basketball game was long over, but it was still affecting me. And as a result, I had pushed away someone who was trying to help. It really is something to pretend you don't want what you know you need for the sake of not wanting to show that you need it.

Venting the frustration of playing terribly and booting out Doc, I walked past the laundry room door and without a second thought, *Bam!* I punched it with everything I had. The innocent door gave, and little wooden pieces splattered all over the floor. I stood, shell shocked. Just as quickly as I swung, I came to my senses. *You are dead wrong, you know that?* Surveying the battleground, I hung my head and sighed. *Dang*! I knew what I had to do as I eyed the spinning dryer through the four-inch hole in the door.

"Doc?"

"Hey, buddy," my friend replied at the other end of the line.

"Could you please come back up?"

"Sure. Be there in a minute."

When Doc's eyes landed at the maimed door, he chuckled. "Did you do this?"

I nodded, my grin as sheepish as a kid who'd just been caught doodling on his bedroom wall with a permanent marker. "I'm ready to talk."

We talked well into the early hours of the morning. I never felt condemned or ashamed when talking to Doc. He kept reminding me that failure is not final. That I had a lion on the inside of me, and one day the world would hear that lion roar. Our relationship was solidifying, and nights like these were the reason why. I liked to hear Doc speak. It wasn't because he always said what I wanted to hear. Doc often shared hard truths I needed to hear and think about. Like Who life really was all about. My focus remained on me and my game and not the One who gave me the gift to play it. Doc reminded me to trust the process—not just the process of becoming a better basketball player but the continued process of growing in my relationship with Christ. It was that relationship that would truly free me on the court. He told me I was great and had nothing to be ashamed of. That God loves me for me, and I should be able to rest in that truth without drifting into condemnation.

By the time Doc left, I shook off the dust from the game and threw out the splintered pieces of wood. And when my alarm went off a few hours later, the past was the past, and I was ready for my next at bat.

The season continued with highs and lows. I'd try to keep my mind centered after bad games, but it was a struggle. This one conversation between Doc and I looped throughout the season.

"You think you let people or your family down?" he'd prod.

"Yeah."

"You think you let God down?"

I'd nod in response.

Enter truth-laden ministering, Doc style. "Well, you didn't. You didn't let your family down or anyone or God down from a game. And if you think you did, I'm going to make clear to you, that's not the kind of God you serve or the kind of people that love you. Unconditional love is not tested when everything is good; it's tested when everything is bad."

Growing up I didn't realize my parents were trying to teach me that truth by taking me to church as a boy. It was their way of pointing me to God's unconditional love. Now I can say with absolute certainty that those seeds from my early childhood were blossoming in my growing understanding of God's love for me.

Throughout the season, Doc would text me Bible verses. There was one in particular he challenged me to study: 1 John 4:18 (NKJV), which says, "Perfect love casts out fear. And the one who fears has not been made perfect in love." Once I really understood it, I'd walk in it, he'd say. I'd come to understand the scripture meant that fear doesn't come from God. God is love. And when you find rest in the fact that God's love for you is perfect, in spite of your achievement or failure, you're freed from fearing the outcome of your endeavor. When we trust God's love and that love shown through His followers, we have nothing to fear. This truth, much easier said than realized, began to chip away at my fears little by little. Instead of condemning myself after I somehow missed the mark, on or off the court, I increasingly rested in the fact that I was loved by God and those around me.

Acknowledging my need for unconditional love exposed something else: my own hypocrisy. I remembered my own lack of love for the one pastor who publicly acknowledged his failure back when I attended FSU. At the time, I used him as a scapegoat to justify my distance from the Church and my disdain for church leaders. But I was wrong. The more I could identify my own shortcomings, the more I saw myself in the shortcomings of others.

It's best said that we all fall short of God's perfect glory every second of every day. The people we see preaching behind pulpits, the idols in society we long to emulate, the man or woman that looks like they have it all together, and the person looking back at you in the mirror are all in need of what only God can give—grace. And if we all need it, who am I to act like I don't? That's not to say we shouldn't hold each other accountable, but it is to understand you handle people the way you'd want to be handled. Doc puts it like this, "You never say what you wouldn't do, you always say, 'But by the grace of God.'" In other words, if it wasn't for God's bountiful grace, we just might be doing a lot of the things we judge other people for.

During a break in my second year with the Magic, I visited Coach Gates at FSU. I even stopped by the church Amanda had brought me to that I swore I'd never come back to. I enjoyed and took to heart the pastor's sermon. Little by little.

CALLING IT OUT

When the team hit the road on February 9, 2019, we cruised past Milwaukee 103-83. I took home seventeen points, six boards, two steals, and two blocks in thirty-one minutes. The very next day we beat the Atlanta Hawks 124-108. I pulled in another seventeen points, two steals, and five blocks. We played in New Orleans two days later and crushed the Pelicans 118-88. I dropped twenty points, seven boards, and three blocks that game. To end the stretch, I put up sixteen points, six boards, a block, and a steal against Charlotte on Valentine's Day. My success on the court was growing.

As the season progressed toward its end, Doc implored me to create the habit of speaking the Word. He'd always remind me in moments of fear, frustration, and doubt to speak back out loud so my ears could hear it to negate thoughts with the Word. Not because words are magic, but because words are powerful. And just like hearing encouraging words when you're down can lift you up, speaking life in a negative situation can change the tenor of your thoughts. For instance, if you're afraid, declare that God is with you (Psalm 118:6). If you're depressed about a situation or from a broken heart, remind yourself that God is near the brokenhearted (Psalm 34:18), and weeping doesn't last forever! To me, reciting scripture is better than any positive statement about how amazing and capable I am. Scripture points me to how amazing and capable God is.

The first time I remember reciting scripture was half-time against the Miami Heat on March 26, 2019. There were about seven games left in the season, and making the playoffs was a real possibility for us. A mark we had no chance of hitting the year before. The game was a disaster right out of the gate. In five minutes, Miami butchered us in a 14-5 lead. For the whole first half, we hung around like wounded dogs.

The night before, Doc had texted me 2 Corinthians 12:9:

> "And He said to me, 'My [God's] grace is sufficient for you, for My strength is made perfect in weakness.' Therefore, most gladly I will rather boast in my infirmities, that the power of Christ may rest upon me."

As we made it back to the locker room during halftime, everyone was frustrated. Including me. It was a big game for us. I sat in my chair, threw my head back, and covered my face with a towel. I began to mumble, "Your grace is sufficient for me, Your strength is made perfect in my weakness." Over and over and over again.

Just as my feet hit the floor at the start of the second half, fear left. I believed that God had me and wasn't going to let me fall. I hit my first shot and a burst of confidence surged through me. Eleven out of my nineteen points came in the second half. We won the game 104-99, positioning our team into the number eight spot in the Eastern Conference standings.

We made the playoffs, which was a huge deal for the city of Orlando. I did fairly well for my first playoff experience. Everything was looking up for me personally and the team for next season. One night Takita surprised me with a real Larry O'Brien trophy engraved "NBA most valuable player 2019-2020 Jonathan Isaac. We believe in you." I wasn't the MVP of the league, but I sure did feel like it. Shortly after the season was over, I asked her to be my girlfriend. I learned so much in season two—about myself, God, and what it meant to walk in faith with like-minded people. Year three looked nothing but promising.

CHAPTER 8

THE HEART OF A LION

GOING INTO THE SUMMER after season two, I was at a place mentally, physically, and spiritually that I'd never been in my life. My body was healthy after a season of playing more games than I missed, and I had an entire summer to develop my skills on the court before my third season. I was growing in peace about where I was headed as a ball player and as a man. I found strength from a growing belief in my heart that everything I'd experienced up to this point had a purpose, and I knew I would continue the journey of finding out what that purpose was.

I started to see myself as not just Jonathan Isaac the basketball player but Jonathan Isaac the man of faith who played basketball. I felt free in that distinction and started to use my various platforms on social media to share my newfound strength. I'd post Bible verses and quotes from Christian philosophers that I'm sure would catch my followers off guard, since my social media presence had been strictly ball before then. Being in a place of confidence about who I was becoming as a person was such a milestone, all I wanted to do that summer was build on that confidence. I got the chance when Bishop asked me if I wanted to travel with the church to Trinidad for their annual global food festival. It's a grand festival where the church prepares food based on the different ethnicities of its members and serves the local people in the destination country. It's a way for the locals to experience cuisines they've never had. The church also brings music, fashion, loads of free clothes and aid, and, most importantly, fellowship with the people.

I said yes, and within a few weeks I was off with the church to Trinidad. I tried to help with everything—preparing food, putting clothes and shoes together to give away, promoting the event, etc. I even MC'd a little bit the day of the festival and interviewed some of the Trinidadians that attended. It really was a blast.

On one of the last days we were there, I posted a video from my hotel room on Instagram. I think it was the first video of me looking and talking directly into a camera that I'd shot in my entire life, and definitely the first I had ever posted online. I was always uncomfortable being on camera. In the video, I talked about my experience in Trinidad and how it was the culmination of choices to follow Christ that led me here. Choices that, at the time,

I didn't know would have a dramatically beneficial impact on my life. I just made up my mind and followed. Looking into the camera of my phone, I implored others to make those same choices. The video shot to 70,000 views in a week. I felt a growing awareness that maybe my calling would take me beyond the basketball court.

I progressed through the summer alongside Bishop, my girlfriend Takita, and more opportunities to let faith beat fear. But the truth is that we never stop growing. Whether faith beats fear in our lives depends on which one we choose to listen to.

During this summer, Bishop challenged me to preach another message on a Sunday. He had asked me to lead a Friday night Bible study earlier in the summer, but it had been over a year since I had spoken on a Sunday. This time I hadn't gotten some download in the middle of the night about what to say. I would have to study and share what stood out to me. I felt a familiar fear over how people would receive me. *I play in the NBA. I'm not relatable. What would Doc think if I went up there and froze? What would Takita think? Can I do this, again?* In the back of my mind, I had written off my first time speaking as it-was–bad-but-because-it-was-my-first-time-everyone-pretended-to-enjoy-it. The thought of going up there again on a Sunday scared me.

One thing Doc had taught me and I had experienced firsthand was that faith is a battle. Fear speaks, loudly and obnoxiously. And for so much of my life, it was the only thing I listened too. My default thought was always the worst case scenario. But now I had a new tool to combat the lies of fear. I wasn't defenseless. I could use faith to speak back. Was I relatable as an NBA player? Maybe not on the surface, but no matter how much you have or how popular you are, life happens to everyone. Wealth is not a cure for fear and anxiety. In most cases, wealth is a mask of peace to hide the real chaos. What was relatable was that I wanted to become a better version of myself, and getting behind the pulpit again was a way to challenge my fears and continue to grow. What would Bishop think if I went up there and froze? How about Takita? The truth is, he'd remind me that I'm not alone and that he wouldn't ask me if he didn't feel I was capable. And Takita would say what she always said, "You're not a mighty man of faith because you're perfect, you're one because you try."

I titled my message on Sunday morning August 25, "Misunderstanding vs. Understanding." In a nutshell I talked about how important it is to really understand something, especially when that something has major implications on who you are or who you could be. To misunderstand what would help you is a tragedy, and that's what I had done up until that night in the car with Doc when he set me straight about what my real problem was (me). I thought that God was trying to take something from me, misunderstanding that he wanted to give something to me—the relationship with Him that would usher me into who I was created to be. I stressed that if we could truly understand the intentions of God toward us, we wouldn't settle for other things that could never satisfy. After this second time speaking, I noticed something important. If I could have seen the end from the beginning, I wouldn't have been afraid in the first place. But because I can't, I have to rely on trusting God who does. My fears, although understandable, weren't a true reflection of my reality. And if I gave in to them, I would have forfeited everything that went right because of everything that could've gone wrong. I walked away understanding that God could walk me through any situation I was willing to trust Him in.

As the summer closed and I now understood my purpose wasn't about me but what God wanted to do through me, I breezed through another Media Day, training camp, and preseason. There still wasn't much camaraderie between me and my teammates, but I was managing. If Doc was right, what I still had to work on and how I'd grown would both be evident in my performance on the court in season three.

A ROAR EMERGED

In the third game of the season, we were set to play Toronto at their house on October 29, 2019. It was the same team that knocked us out of the playoffs the season before. Midway through my second year with the Magic, I started the tradition of calling Doc and praying before every game. Before this particular game in Toronto, he prayed and said, "Remember, the righteous are as bold as lions." That's from Proverbs 28:1, but I didn't know it at the time. This was a bit before I fell in love with lions. I learned that Jesus was the "Lion of the tribe of Judah" and thought it was cool.

Thing about a lion is that he doesn't need to go around telling everyone he's a lion. He doesn't need to growl or roar to affirm his status. His confidence is deeply rooted in who he is. He never forgets it. The righteous can be as bold as lions because their righteousness doesn't come from how good they are but from how good God is. A lion would later become my screen saver.

I went into the game reciting, "The righteous are as bold as lions." It was the best game I had played in my NBA career. I sank three threes in the first quarter and went on to score my career high at that time with twenty-four points along with seven boards and three blocks. Whenever there was a timeout or I was on the bench, I would recite under my breath, "The righteous are as bold as lions." In that game I'd go back on to the court with more courage than I had when I stepped off of it. They weren't just words to me. They were alive, fueling me with belief. God was right there with me, and I wasn't righteous because of how good I was but because of how good He is. No shame, no anxiety, no fear.

I was excited. If I stayed healthy and continued to play with confidence, the future was limitless. Still reeling from the adrenaline spike after the win, I texted Doc, "I believe." I meant it. The game was a sign that I had grown in confidence through the summer. But a moment of belief was something I'd already accomplished inside and outside of the game. Continued growth for me in season three would be maintaining belief that I was great, even when things didn't look so good—because, c'mon now, how many athletes have a great game every time? The next game I scored ten points, as the familiar pressure I'd put on myself mounted and weighed me down. I found myself right back where I started. Doubting myself and doubting if God was with me.

I'd score eleven points the next game and seven points in the game after that. Bishop and Takita were there with their usual encouragement. I witnessed growth in my ability to snap out of my old habits and not dwell on disappointment. With a clear head, I'd roar again. Just a few days later, I scored twenty points. Let me be clear. It wasn't that I had to score twenty points every game; it was that I knew I was capable of so much more than I offered when I'd succumb to fear. And I was intent on facing it.

MINISTER OF DEFENSE

A few games after scoring twenty-two points, we faced off against the Indiana Pacers on their turf. We were two games under .500, which was a great start to a season about twenty games in. I prayed with Doc as usual before the game started and went into it feeling encouraged. I had a great game hitting a new career high of twenty-five points. I also chipped in two blocks, four steals, and nine boards. I was elated to see my growing potential in the league, but this time was different from my last career-high game. I'll never forget as the game got closer to the wire, and even as I scored point after point, I felt fear creep its way into my head. I messaged Doc after the game, "I'm still afraid." Sure, I had a new career high, but I wasn't completely free. Doc texted me back, saying, "I know. But you did great! It's a process." He knew much better than I did that any personal process, no matter how much you've grown, isn't fully accomplished overnight.

Something was happening so far this season that I hadn't paid attention to. I was leading the league in blocked shots and was eleventh in steals. What was my best season ever in almost every category so far was manifest by the possibility and desire of our fans for me to be selected Defensive Player of the Year. I was even gifted the nickname Minister of Defense by our announcers for my love for God and swatting shots. I loved it, and my defensive prowess gained national attention rapidly. The more people talked about it, the more I cared about protecting my status as Minster of Defense. I would check the leader boards as me and Anthony Davis traded number one and two spots after each game.

One of my best defensive games of the season so far was against the Dallas Mavericks on their court. This game would be my first time matching up against the highly touted Kristaps Porziņģis. There was anticipation from the fans on how my defense would fair against his ability to shoot the deep ball at seven feet tall. I finished the game with a stat line of thirteen points, six blocks, four steals, five assists, and ten rebounds. It was considered the best defensive game of the season so far. I was only the third player in NBA history to amass that stat line, joining Hall of Famers Hakeem Olajuwon and Ralph Sampson. I put up three-plus blocks fourteen times in thirty games and had a game against the Milwaukee Bucks where I recorded seven steals. One of my teammates described me as a lion in a giraffe's body.

The lion in me wasn't just showing up on the court but pregame too, signifying the growth I experienced in the summer. Our team was only getting better, and reaching higher than an eighth seed was looking more and more of a reality.

Just as I still had room to grow in battling fear on the court, I had room to grow in battling fear off of it—mainly with my teammates. There's always been something in me that longed for the brotherhood I experienced with the team at ISB, with CJ, and with the group at FSU. In those times, we were all so much alike in our experiences and desires. We all wanted to get as far with basketball as we could and have as much fun along the way as possible. But the NBA was different, and I was different. Only now I was comfortable with being different.

Our team had a routine of always praying the "Our Father" prayer together before we would run out onto the court. I think most teams do it as a symbol of respect. Sometimes as I prayed along in the background, the thought would come that I should ask them if I could pray instead. Every time the thought arose, I'd excuse it with, *They'll probably say no,* or, *I wouldn't know what to pray.* Until one day when I didn't let the excuses stop me.

Right before the same teammate initiated the familiar, "Our Father who art in heaven," I blurted out, "Hey, you guys mind if I just said a quick prayer, instead of the 'Our Father'?" Everyone's eyes turned toward me. "Go ahead," the player who would usually lead the prayer said. I took a deep breath, and with surety I prayed, "God, thank you for this day and the ability you've given us to play the game that we love. Help us to play hard, unafraid, and untied. Keep us from harm and give us the win, in Jesus name I pray."

When I said "amen" and looked up, the scene around me was frozen.

"Yo, JI," one of my teammates burst out, "Did you just pray that off the top of your head?"

"Yeah," I replied with a laugh.

"That's crazy bro," a teammate shouted, nodding his head in approval.

After a "family on three—one, two, three, family!!!" we took off through the tunnel.

From that night on, me praying turned into a thing. Up until my season three ended, leading prayer was my job. I'll never forget I missed two quick games nursing a tweaked ankle. I walked into the locker room from a shower as the team headed out to huddle up. Just as I was drying my fro, a teammate busted into the locker room and started yelling, "JI! JI! Let's go, bro! You got to pray!" I laughed, and while still soaked and in my towel, I thanked God and prayed for a win. We won.

For me it wasn't the prayer that was profound but that what Bishop told me was true. I was experiencing "as it is in life, so is it on the court." I was seeing myself evolve right before my own eyes.

DETOUR TIME

Just like that, on the first of January 2020, two games after I scored nineteen points against the Bucks, it all came to a halt. We were in Washington playing the Wizards. I hit a baseline turnaround jumper to kick things off. Within a few moments, I stole the ball and was charging toward the Wizards' basket. I euro-stepped right to left and stepped on an opposing player's foot. My knee jerked outward and

I collapsed in a world of pain. I clutched my knee thinking this is what it had to feel like to tear your ACL.

That New Year's Day, I didn't hear the cheering crowd as I was carried on a gurney through a tunnel to the underbelly of the arena; I just heard the throbbing pulse in my knee. A doctor tugged on my knee in different directions to see if there was any give. With a few nods and looks at our head trainer, he concluded he didn't feel any structural damage but wouldn't know for sure until a proper MRI. I let out a sigh of relief for my ACL but knew something had to be wrong for my knee to feel as bad as it did.

I sat alone in the locker room with ice on my knee, watching the team play on a TV. I was so frustrated at myself and even God as I tried to contemplate why this happened. *Why now? Why when everything is going great and I'm growing and feeling as if I'm doing as best as I can? What did I do wrong*?

I called Doc. "I think I hurt my knee."

"What are they saying?"

"That they won't really know anything for sure until I get back home and get an MRI."

"Okay, how are YOU doing?"

"I don't understand why I got hurt again. It doesn't make any sense."

Doc slowly replied, "All things work together for the good, Jonathan. I don't have an answer for you as to why, but rest in the fact that God does. He sees from a perspective that me and you can't. He sees the end from the beginning, remember." I took a deep breath over the phone but remained otherwise silent. "This is a part of your journey in trusting Him. If you knew He was with you at your highest, know that He's with you in your lowest. He's a God of the hills and the valleys. Maybe that's what He's trying to teach you, that He has a plan and if you could trust Him in this, you could trust Him in anything."

"You're right, Doc. I trust Him."

Back in Orlando, and an MRI later, it turned out my ACL was intact. That was the good news. The bad news was that I had partially torn my biceps femoris, which is part of a group of three muscles that make up a hamstring and connect in the back corner of the knee. The game plan was to wear a cast over pretty much my entire leg for a few weeks to let things settle down and start healing, then transition into a brace that was locked out at full extension. The goal was not to bend it or bear any weight early on, so crutches were going to be my best friends.

When I shared the news with Bishop, he said enthusiastically, "Okay! We've taken this test before! You just focus on healing up and getting back on the court. You have your family. Takita can drop off food and make sure you're good. You have me and your church family. You're gonna get through this and come back better than ever."

This unexpected detour left me mopish for just a few days after it all happened. I decided to go by the church one night and just sit at the alter with my leg all casted up. I reassured myself that God had a purpose for what He allows and that I was going to trust Him through this process. I'd come back better, like I did after my rookie season.

With a clear head, I took my attention off my knee that needed time to heal and put it on whatever God had next. Our church has its own TV channel (JGNtv.org). Back in the summer after season two, Doc had encouraged me to take a stab at starting my own show on the channel. Takita came up with the name "Judah Nation," to give viewers an inside look at the Judah off the court. I'd share about my faith and encourage others to embark on the journey of becoming who God created them to be alongside me. I was drenched in sweat from the anxiety of filming my first episode, but it got easier, and felt more natural every episode after that. It was so weird but humbling to hear people share how they saw me on TV and were encouraged and helped by the messages and thought I should continue doing it. So throughout the summer I did. Once the season started, though, recording took a back seat, with little free time. The day after I sat at the altar, I recorded a video encouraging anyone going through a storm they didn't understand. One thing I said has stuck with me: "Maybe God allows us to go through difficult times so we can identify with others going through difficult times." In that moment, I could speak to anyone about trusting God because that's exactly what I was doing in order to keep going.

On March 1 of 2020, me and Takita and a few other members of the church became ordained ministers. Doc felt it was fitting, as I'd spoken at the church several times. Now I really was the Minister of Defense.

I kept a positive outlook on my situation as my knee began to bend and heal. My eyes were on the future, not looking back to what could have or should have been. Evidence of my focus on the future came in my elaborate plan to whisk Takita (and both our families) abroad to the City of Love for an engagement surprise. Knowing the woman Takita is and experiencing how supportive and helpful she was during the early stagnant stages of my rehab, I knew she was the one for me.

Just as I was making hotel reservations and buying plane tickets, something we never saw coming changed the world. At 12:26 p.m. on March 11, 2020, the World Health Organization declared COVID-19 a global pandemic. An hour-and-a-half later, the Golden State Warriors announced plans to play their scheduled game against the Brooklyn Nets the following day, but minus the fans. At 8:26 p.m. the same day, just before tip-off between the Utah Jazz and the Oklahoma Thunder, officials informed both coaches that Jazz center Rudy Gobert had tested positive for COVID. The game was immediately canceled. Minutes later, the NBA announced the suspension of the rest of the 2018-2019 season.

All of my plans for a movie-like engagement were shattered in a day. And on top of that, there was no more basketball to watch. I decided to make the best of the situation. I proposed to Takita on May 2, 2020, after turning the rooftop of my building into a makeshift Paris with lights, seven-foot Eiffel towers, a red carpet, and a huge Welcome-to-Paris balloon arch. Her "yes" sealed our fate.

Whispers were going around of a potential NBA Bubble in the making. My eyes were set on a season-three comeback, with extra time to heal before the games resumed. Maybe this was all part of a bigger plan after all.

CHAPTER 9

THE STAND

SOON AFTER THE NBA'S ANNOUNCEMENT about suspending the season, the Magic's front office gathered us all for a meeting to debrief the situation. No one on staff could answer any questions related to the season, but a doctor had been brought in to address any medical-related queries and explain what was known about COVID at the time. I remember the doctor giving us some fairly simple advice; washing your hands periodically, being mindful of touching your face, and avoiding large crowds would give you the best chance of escaping sure death. I'm joking, but there was definitely a dramatic mood that descended when speaking about COVID. Like as soon as it became the topic of conversation, intense gloomy music would start playing in the background as your breathing shallowed, making you think you might just have it. Only one thing stood out to me from the meeting with the doctor. It was his nonchalant affirmation that masks were of little to no use at stopping the spread of COVID. His explanation that COVID particles were small enough to pass through most masks made sense but left me perplexed as to why we were all handed masks before entering the meeting.

At the time, the Centers for Disease Control and Prevention and the World Health Organization advised that masks should be saved for sick people and health care workers, who were already in an overburdened medical environment with an emaciated supply of PPE (personal protection equipment). Of course, these same organizations flipped the script the following month, recommending cloth masks and then double masking. But I'm getting ahead of myself.

Life as we knew it? Interrupted. Still, none of us in the room that day, neither players nor physicians, could anticipate the enormous implications this virus would have for years to come. We were told to stay home and stay in shape, and we'd be updated if anything with the league changed. I detected a hint of dread in the unknowing tone of the directions. On the other hand, not knowing anything about COVID at this point, I saw an opportunity to lock in on my rehab and make a possible comeback if fate allowed it. The team sent over equipment, like free weights and a bike, and instructions for a daily workout, to keep me busy.

MESSAGES, MOVEMENTS, AND MOTION

Darnella Frazier was seventeen years old when she captured the video of George Floyd's death on May 25, 2020. The video, shared on social media the next day, went viral, sparking global outrage. Anger had already been brewing over the shooting of Breonna Taylor on March 13 and multiple other incidents of alleged police brutality and racism. National protests erupted. It wasn't just your social-justice-minded neighbor who got involved. Everyone, it seemed, was on board and outraged. Average citizens, celebrities, political figures, and athletes locked arms and condemned police violence against blacks and demanded structural changes.

The video of George Floyd's death was awful to watch. There was a pit in my stomach as he cried out. Understandably, the response to that video reached deafening levels. And I, too, could articulate my disgust at racism, having experienced it. Although the strong feelings of the country felt justified, what made me pause was the question, "What is the right way to respond?" Where does Jonathan Isaac, and all of his experiences, fit into such a tragic moment? What's next?

Black Lives Matter, a global organization demanding equality and an end to racism, was everywhere. I was aware of the organization from prior events, but if you hadn't heard of them before, you did now. Every social media post and headline unrelated to COVID proclaimed BLACK

LIVES MATTER, words that, at face value, I agreed with. But there was a narrative behind the words that I disagreed with. Behind the altruistic title BLM, the narrative that the organization advanced was that now is the time for aggravated social and political action in defense of black lives. Their narrative drew a bitter line in the sand: us against them. You're either with us or against us. It was angry, vengeful, and tribal, even as it was wrapped in an understandable passion for the marginalized, which I shared. I knew BLM wasn't a message I was comfortable cosigning, but I was unsure of how or where to lend my voice, or if I needed to speak at all.

As BLM lead the way, protests continued. Some protests turned violent and resulted in rioting and the destruction of property and businesses. Doc preached a message around this time, sharing that we could help heal the nation if we would show God's love toward our perceived enemies, rather than letting our heightened emotions lead. The scripture he used is from Matthew 26, where Jesus is arrested while with His disciples and later innocently sentenced to death by crucifixion. As those sent by the chief priests and elders lunged at Jesus to take Him into custody, Peter drew his sword and sliced off the ear of one of the capturers. Peter may have been the kind of guy you want on your side in a street fight, but Jesus disagreed with Peter's reaction. Jesus told Peter, and in effect, all of us, "Put your sword away. Anyone who lives by fighting will die by fighting" (Matthew 26:52). In other words, what you're fighting for will be lost in the perpetual scuffle. Doc explained that he wouldn't blame Peter for his reaction in the moment of possibly losing someone dear to him. Although Peter's violence was understandably human, it would only hinder what Jesus was trying to accomplish. Jesus went on to heal His captor's ear. Doc ended by quoting John 13:35, "By this will all men know that you're my disciples, if you love one another." Hearing Doc's "love wins" message through the lens of a Bible story shaped how I saw myself in the fight for change.

When I looked at my life, encompassing all of my shortcomings, failures, and hypocrisy, what stood out was that I was just like everyone else. Depravity is the unifying characteristic of mankind. If there was anybody that could point their finger at others for their sin, it was Jesus. But He never did. Instead, He showed love to His enemies and invited them to receive understanding.

As I reviewed my own story, I realized it's been the love of God and people, seeing past my dysfunction, that has helped groom me into the man that I am becoming. Maybe if both black and white people could see their own faults and not just the faults in others, there could be change. Maybe the answer is loving someone past their moral failures because you've failed morally too. That was the message of love I experienced and wanted to share.

During the height of COVID and BLM, J.U.M.P. Ministries Global Church launched "Ready, Set, Feed," a program Doc created to provide breakfast and lunch to kids in poor communities who would usually depend on school for food. With schools being closed, Doc knew that many kids, and families for that matter, would go without. We sprang into action, delivering over 20,000 meals to our communities over a three-month span. My fiancé, Takita, and a team from J.U.M.P. went door to door, fully masked and adhering to CDC guidelines as much as possible of course, delivering food, meeting kids, and spreading hope in what seemed like a hopeless situation.

As time passed, I continued my rehab, progressing from my apartment back to the arena as whispers of a resurrected season spread. I worked tirelessly day in and day out while promising my trainers that I'd be ready. They were skeptical, but if I reached my sprint, strength, and load markers, the decision to play would be up to me.

THE BUBBLE

On July 7, twenty-two out of thirty NBA teams checked into the famous Disney Bubble, created in the ESPN Wide World of Sports Complex at the Walt Disney World Resort in Orlando. The goal was to create a COVID-free space to continue the season. Teams would have a couple exhibition games that didn't count to give guys a chance to get their legs under them. Real games would start on July 30 and would be played in three different arenas. No fans were allowed, and the stands were filled only with limited media, inactive players, team executives, and NBA personnel. The Bubble was decked out with a players-only lounge, barbers and hair stylists, and whatever the Disney grounds had to offer—from golf courses to fishing excursions. Teams would stay in three different hotels on the campus: the Grand Floridian where we stayed, the Yacht Club, and the Gran Destino Tower at Coronado Springs. This was home away from home for at least six weeks or, for some teams, up to three months.

I was cleared to play in our last "fake" game against the Denver Nuggets before things got real. I was so excited to be taking the court again, and there was a lot of anticipation around my return. Only being allowed to play seven minutes, I put up thirteen points and two steals, which erupted social media. Magic fans were happy I was back before the playoffs, which would occur later in the bubble. My eyes were set on the next game. The real game.

But the bubble was more than just protection from a virus; the bubble became a megaphone for activism. In fact, it quickly became known as the social justice bubble. Upon arrival, the Toronto Raptors rode in on a black bus with "Black Lives Matter" painted on the side. We got word that same phrase would be placed on the three playing courts in the bubble. Players wore shoes and jerseys with names and phrases on them including

"George Floyd," "Say her name," "How many more," "Ready for Change," and "Black Lives Matter." This police brutality issue was of particular importance in a league that was predominately black.

There was an unspoken pressure to prove your allegiance to the BLM movement. To be silent was to deny the value of black lives. People and organizations scrambled to outdo each other to obtain the coveted label "ally." Everyone feared being labeled racist. Days into being in the bubble, our coach had us watch *Good Trouble*, the documentary about U.S. Representative John Lewis and his six decades committed to activism. The film itself was inspiring. Lewis was remarkable. But there was a subtle awkwardness shared among the group from being forced to view such a film at this moment in time.

There was one topic related to social justice that surged through the early weeks of the bubble and only got louder as games were in sight: kneeling for the national anthem. Four years earlier, on September 1, San Francisco 49ers' quarterback Colin Kaepernick took his first knee protesting systemic racism in America. The question in the bubble was, "Is kneeling the right thing to do?" That question was answered for most of the players on the evening of July 30, when the New Orleans Pelicans facing the Utah Jazz kneeled for the national anthem, along with coaches and referees. Followed by the Los Angeles Clippers against the Lakers. All wearing Black Lives Matter T-shirts. No teams had knelt during the exhibition games, so there wasn't any pressure before now. But my team was scheduled to play the following day against the Brooklyn Nets. Whether we would kneel or not was front and center.

We had a team meeting after the Pelicans/Jazz game was played. Everyone was there—players, coaches, and staff. The message was clear but frantic, "If you guys want to take a knee during the anthem, we support it. Just whatever you decide, do it together. We'll leave just the players in here and you all decide." As coaches and staff cleared, the room trembled with affirming statements of, "There's not a choice to make here. We have to kneel," and, "We can't be the first team to not take a knee." The consensus was obvious. Of course, we were going to kneel. There wasn't a conversation to be had.

I remained silent the entire time. *That's the problem,* my mind reeled. *Who said this was the only way to support black lives?* One of my teammates locked eyes with me and said, "Yo, Jonathan, what do you think of all this?"

Crickets. Everyone in the room gave me their attention. I swallowed and gathered myself. "Y'all, I'm not going to kneel or wear that T-shirt."

Vocal chaos ensued. "If we don't do this together, tomorrow is going to be crazy," one teammate said, throwing up his hands. From there it was hard to hear anything as side conversations broke out and one guy shouted over the other.

As the reality of my decision not to kneel set in, one teammate grabbed his belongings and shouted, “Look, JI is not going to kneel. It is what it is. Everybody else do what you want,” and he left. With nothing more to add, everyone else grabbed their things and left too. I stood alone. Again.

NO TURNING BACK

I walked back to my hotel room, slowly. Contemplating what not kneeling would really mean. *Am I going to be able to handle this?* I pondered under the dark velvet sky. My teammate who said tomorrow would be crazy was absolutely right.

I called Doc as I lay in bed that night. We had talked about the protests and everything, but I’d never told him that I’d made a decision about kneeling.

“The team is going to kneel tomorrow, and I’m not going to,” I told him point blank.

“Okay. Why? You have to be prepared to answer that question, Jonathan.”

“It’s deeper than skin color,” I began. “We’ve all done wrong—all of us. Racism isn’t the only thing that needs fixing. It’s our hearts. Jesus has been the answer for me, and I believe He’s the answer for the world.”

“Okay, Jonathan, I’m with you. You’re not alone.”

“You don’t understand,” I interrupted. “This is going to be big, Doc. Like front page news big. I don’t sign my contract until next year. I could be out the league. People are getting 'canceled' left and right."

"I know." My friend took a breath. Then he sternly said, "Remember, Jonathan, you cannot stand for God and God not stand for you."

Doc and I prayed to seal the deal. Before I attempted to rest for the night, I made two more phone calls. One to my fiancé, where she echoed Doc's encouragement: "Baby, I am right there with you. Lead the way." The second was to someone in the Magic organization. I wanted to inform the team of my decision out of respect, so they wouldn't be caught off guard.

I barely slept throughout the night. I'd doze off and wake only to check the time and see I'd only been asleep for half an hour. Every time I'd wake up, the first thing on my mind was that I was afraid, and I couldn't go through with it. People would tear me apart. I'd remind myself that I wouldn't be standing alone. That this was bigger than me.

Early in the morning, I had messaged the equipment manager, asking if there was anything for me to wear other than a Black Lives Matter shirt as a warm-up. There wasn't. Before I knew it, we were in the locker room and it was time to dress for the game. I dressed in my sweatpants with nothing over my jersey, sitting in my locker with headphones on staring into space.

After coach gave his standard pregame remarks, it was time to leave the locker room and huddle up before taking the court. My white team jersey stuck out like a jumbo marshmallow in coffee.

One of my teammates looked at me, barely making eye contact. “Yo, J. What are you doing, man?” His voice was low, his tone soft.

I shrugged. What else could I say? Pretty much everyone else acted as if I wasn’t there.

Going through the layup lines before the game, I felt settled. Confident. I made my moves and just focused on what I knew in my heart changed me. As the only one not wearing a BLM shirt in the arena, I felt the hot stares of the other team and the NBA personnel around the court. I kept running and shooting, trying to stay focused.

As the pregame clock wound down, I could feel my heartbeats stronger and stronger through my chest. Then, like the seconds ticking away before a lethal injection, a sobering feeling of reality washed over me. The buzzer sounded, and it was time to line up for the national anthem.

Players shuffled to their positions, one by one dropping their knees to the floor. Some of the players locked arms with others beside them. Except for the 6’11” Magic forward who towered above the line. My feet firmly planted, I bowed my head. *Purify my motives*, I prayed. Nerves relaxed, oxygen flowing freely throughout my body. Each second that passed as the woman on the jumbo screen sang, I relaxed more. I was realizing that this was really happening.

The song ended, and it was game time. I noticed the same confused stares as I made my way to our bench. Once the game started, standing was the furthest thing from my mind.

We killed it, 128-118. I put up sixteen points and six rebounds in sixteen minutes of play. Game over.

But really, of course, it was just the beginning.

POST-GAME PRESS CONFERENCE

When the final buzzer sounded, my attention flipped from our first win since the season restart, to what the post-game press conference would entail. In all honesty, I was nervous. I wondered about the "Uncle Tom" and "coon" conclusions people may have already made about me before I had a chance to speak. After changing clothes, I was escorted toward the Zoom media room. On the way there, several people looked as if they knew what I was about to go through and felt sorry for me. When I finally made it, I took my seat and a deep breath.

The first reporter nosedived to the stand. "I have a two-part question for you. So you didn't kneel during the anthem, but you also didn't wear a Black Lives Matter shirt. Do you believe that Black lives matter?"

Of course I believed that black lives matter! But I was ignorantly stunned by her question. Being a black man, I didn't think I would need to justify the value of my own life. But in that moment, being black wasn't enough. Being black didn't hold as much solidarity as wearing a T-shirt. Kneeling for the anthem to symbolize support for black lives was no symbol at all; it was an order. And my allegiance to the cause was measured solely by my obedience to that command.

I answered her question by saying, "I didn't feel that putting that shirt on and kneeling went hand in hand with supporting black lives. My life has been supported by the Gospel, and that's the message I want to share."

"Everyone is made in the image of God, and we all fall short of His glory. We can point fingers at each other about whose evil is worse, but that just comes down to whose evil is most visible. The Gospel of Jesus Christ is that there is grace for us all, and if we could recognize that we are no better than another, we could get past not only racism but everything else that plagues our society."

The press conference sped past in a blur. I tried to answer each question as transparently as I could. It was difficult given the circumstances and knowing that every word would be scrutinized. I understood that what I was advocating wasn't an easy thing to receive or put into immediate action. To forgive someone's wrongdoing goes against every fiber of our being. But that's exactly why we need God. Because God forgives us for our wrong, we can forgive others for theirs. That goes for both sides.

The last question of the press conference was about the country: "Jonathan, your decision—did it have anything to do with the thought of patriotism?"

I felt I knew where this question was leading. Any hint of love for America would be perceived as love for her imperfect history and not respect for her progress.

But my love for America—or lack thereof—didn't influence my decision. I simply couldn't echo the spirit of the BLM movement. I'm grateful to live in a free country where the right to protest or not protest is protected. Like any country filled with people who aren't perfect, America isn't perfect. Doc would say from time to time as encouragement, "You haven't done everything right, but you haven't done everything wrong either." That, in my opinion, is what is being lost in discussing the nature of the country.

As I walked back to the hotel, familiar stares of inquisitiveness met me along the way. One gentleman stopped me and said he wanted to shake my hand because he heard me loud and clear. When I was inside my hotel room, I finally had the chance to look at my phone, which had been blowing up since the game ended. I saw tweets brandishing terms like "sell out" and "bootlicker." At first that was all my eyes gravitated towards. But after a few minutes, those messages were washed out by a sea of encouragement. Not everybody agreed with what I had to say—I knew that. What I didn't expect was the multitude of people who did agree with me. Within forty-eight hours, my texts were flooded, and my Instagram account went from 90,000 followers to 220,000. People were reaching out to me to say that they either agreed with my message or merely respected the fact that in today's climate I was willing to stand up and share it.

Doc was my first phone call to decompress from the stressful day.

FALLOUT

The next day, while riding the team bus back to the hotel from practice, all the players got a text message about an impromptu players-only meeting. As we exited the bus, a teammate tapped me and said, "Heads up. The meeting is about you."

As everyone shuffled into the meeting room and took a seat, the silence broke with a, "We made a decision to kneel as a team, and it means a lot to some of us. Now we have to waste our time and answer questions about you not kneeling and how we feel about it."

"You're hijacking the movement!" another player blurted out.

It felt like a firing squad.

One of the guys barked, "Well, I refuse to kneel next to him [me]. Next game during the anthem, I'm going to stay in the locker room."

"No, man," another player objected. "We can't change what we're doing. Everyone has to do the same thing, or it's just going to be a bigger story. Are you going to stand again?"

"Yea," I said after a deep exhale.

"Then that's that; everything stays the same."

"No, man! There's black people dying in the streets," the earlier teammate interjected.

I piped up again. "Look, I see the same thing that you guys see and want change just like you. When you all made the decision to kneel, I respected it. I'm just asking for that same respect."

One of the players extended an olive branch. "Listen guys, we know Jonathan. He said what he said during the press conference, and I think he did fine with explaining his position. That's what he believes. We don't have to fight about it. Let's just keep it moving."

Murmurs rippled through the room. Once again, one by one, the players filed out. Before the last teammate left the room, he said, "JI, I understand why you did what you did, and I agree with you. I just don't think people are ready for it."

I nodded and replied. "I hear you. But that doesn't mean it shouldn't be done."

I stayed there for another half hour by myself going over the conversation. I was crushed. I wanted my teammates to understand. I still wanted to be a part of the team. Doubts pushed into my mind from every angle. *Did I handle that right? Should I have said something different?* I know they believe in what they're fighting for, and at face value it looks like I'm going against that. But I want the same thing. I want the world to heal and be a better place. This is just the only way that I can see that actually coming to pass.

Another slow walk to my hotel room. I broke down crying on the phone with Doc as I recounted what had happened. He quieted me and said, "They knelt for what they believe in, and you stood for what you believe in." I hung up the phone, encouraged.

Our next game, on August 2, approached like lightning. This time was nothing like the first. Thoughts of the need to make God and my supporters proud with a great game consumed me. And so did the pressure. We lined up in the same fashion as the national anthem was sung. In no time, the ball was in the air and the game was live. We were killing them, but I was unsatisfied with my hesitant and anxious performance. Late in the game I took an open three, and it clanked against the backboard. Determined to pull it together, I caught the ball off of a throwback and drove toward the lane. I planted with a move called a hop-step and immediately felt my knee twist violently. I tumbled to the floor, clutching my leg to my chest, screaming, "No, no, no, no, no!"

I got wheelchaired to a back room, not even trying to fight the tears. Shortly after, I was assisted onto an MRI truck on-site where I was given the bad news: My ACL was torn.

CHAPTER 10

AFTERMATH

APPARENTLY, STANDING WASN'T ENOUGH FOR ME. Let me explain.

When I played that first game right after choosing to stand for the national anthem, I didn't pack on the pressure. I didn't try and prove who I was on the court. I just played ball and did my best to help the team win. Everything felt natural and free-flowing that game.

But the game in which I tore my ACL was different. I felt it was my responsibility to curb the negativity surrounding my stance and continue to make God and my supporters proud of me by delivering a great performance.

In other words, I got in the way.

As the game slipped into the fourth quarter, I was upset about how poorly I was playing. The funk led me into a hard drive left, trying to force my hand but ultimately leading me to the ground. After Takita drove me home and I explained my thought process to Doc, he made it clear to me that "standing wasn't enough for you." He insisted that I had nothing to prove to anyone after I stood. Not the naysayers or the supporters. He said that God and those that loved me were proud of me long before I stood, and that should have been all that mattered. But it wasn't.

My entire life I've tried to gain the praise of others to validate my worth, and the pressure I took on after the stand brought that to the surface. I tried to carry the burden of a moment bigger than me, and in doing so, I took my eyes off of God and placed them on myself. After the conversation with Doc, I began to realize that this whole time God wasn't trying to make me great so I could finally see myself that way. He wanted me to understand that I was already great in and because of Him, that true greatness is marked by our choice to follow Jesus, not some arbitrary metric of achievement in the world's eyes.

Even though I'd made great progress from my middle school class clown days, I still had plenty of room to grow. Don't we all. This revelation was a big serving of humble pie. I recognized my shortcomings while my injury was being celebrated on social media. Karma, "a knee for a knee," is what many declared. My injury, according to some, was punishment for standing against black lives. The negative remarks didn't bother me. If I've learned anything up until this point, it's that God is good. We have a lot more to do with our current situations than we'd like to admit, but no matter how badly we've messed up, God always offers a way forward. He's not just a God of the hills; He's also a God of the valleys. That's His love. I may had been playing the lead role in my circumstance, which I accepted, but God still held the lead role in my life. And in moments to come, He would prove that He is still with me. Heading into surgery with Takita by my side, I was focused on bouncing back no matter how long it'd take. And, most importantly, finding out the plan that God still had for me.

A HIDDEN OPPORTUNITY

Coming home from surgery was sobering. Accepting round two of being bedridden (only now for longer) and pain meds that kept me dull wasn't easy. With so little to do early in the rehab process and so much time to dwell on my predicament, I could have easily slipped into depression. What kept me motivated were the uplifting presence of Takita, family, and Doc, and the outpouring of love and support from people all over the country. I received thousands of messages on social media and boxes full of encouraging letters from people who wanted me to know they were praying for and standing with me. People who love God and love our country. Even people who just respected the fact I was willing to stand for my beliefs in a time where society made clear that only one belief mattered. My jersey became the second highest selling in the bubble.

One day as I lay across the couch reading letters, Doc came over and excitedly shared that he had a word for me. "You're going to write a book and make a movie!" His words hung in the air for a few moments.

"A book? A movie? Huh?"

"Jonathan, people know your stand, but they don't know your story. Your story is what truly makes the stand profound," Doc explained, "Oh, the glory it would bring to God's name. He's not done with you, Jonathan. You tell people the story of what, or rather Who, changed your life and I promise it'll change theirs. People will understand why you stood!"

"And not just that," Doc added, "but you could impact even the people that disagreed with you. The people who just wanted things to get better and got swept up into the movement. You're giving them the answer that would really change things—Christ! A book first, and then a movie."

I joined in on the excitement as I saw the vision of what the book could be. A story of the journey only a few people knew about.

"Okay! okay!" I said, nodding my head in agreement as we broke out in a dance.

"But wait, how in the world do you write a book?"

"Jonathan," Doc interjected with a smile. "You've got all the time in the world to figure it out while you rehab. Work on your leg and work on the book. You can do it. God always has a plan, and this is a part of it. Your book and movie will outlive you. Your stand for Christ will ripple into eternity!"

"Let's do it," I declared, smirkingly resuming my two-step. "I'll call my agent."

Just like that I found myself buying Microsoft Word, outlining away, and praying that all the right pieces would fall into place to bring a book to life.

MEETING THE POPE

One random day in November 2020, Takita was over dropping off food when I got a phone call from a representative from our players union, the National Basketball Players Association (NBPA). The rep shared that an offer was on the table for me to fly to Rome and meet the Pope. Yes, I said that right, the Pope! The rep explained that he had seen the NBA's efforts to fight against racial injustice and wanted to meet a few players who were willing. Turned out due to last minute planning, not many players were. When my name was suggested as an alternative, there was hesitation; but the offer eventually found me. I told her I'd call her back right away with an answer, then I dialed Doc. We had a laugh over the seemingly ironic situation. Doc felt that I shouldn't pass up the opportunity to share with the Pope the same thing I'd shared in my post-game press conference in the bubble.

Three days after presenting a negative COVID test, I was off on a private jet with four other NBA players and NBPA personnel to Rome. On November 24, 2020, I had the incredible opportunity to shake the Pope's hand and present him with my jersey. Our group of maybe ten people in total had a fifteen-minute sit down with him in which we individually shared a bit about our vision toward racial justice and equality. When it was my turn, I stood and thanked him for the opportunity and talked about how God's kind of love is what was missing, not only from our individual lives but how we interacted with each other. I recited John 3:16 to point to Jesus and the answer God has given for the brokenness in this world and in humanity. A few minutes later, it was over. I may not agree with everything the Pope believes, but I'm glad I was in that room that day. He was down to earth for a man of such great influence.

A few days after making it back to Orlando, I got a call from our team doctor. He informed me that my morning test for COVID had come back positive. The league required every player to test before entering the arena. Results were received from the lab the same day. Hearing I had COVID was weird. I had seen the world halted and turned upside down from something I hadn't experienced. Now I was among the infected and contagious. A sense of embarrassment accompanied the illness due to the widespread panic about how highly transmissible it was. I was to be banished into quarantine for close to two weeks. I experienced light symptoms of fatigue and shortness of breath.

Shortly after I beat COVID, the NBA's shortened season kicked off in December of 2020, without fans. Players and staff were expected to follow intense rules in hopes of everyone getting through the season healthy and unscathed by this virus.

TAKE THE SHOT

As the new year turned and the young season progressed, I was in the background rehabbing, working on this book, and eyeing COVID, which was quickly growing from just a medical situation into the focus of a cultural and political war. So much was happening.

Day after day, new headlines blared of a growing death toll; a different department of society being shut down; and accusatory fingers being pointed in every direction. And, of course, the country's leadership taking on the pandemic had changed. Trump was out, and Biden was in. During the election, the consensus among Democrats was that Trump didn't take the pandemic seriously enough and illegitimately fast-tracked a vaccine that would only make things worse. But once the White House changed hands, the new powers-that-be touted the COVID vaccine as the way to end the pandemic.

I watched as mask mandates, distance protocols, school closures, and other restrictions were implemented to try and manage the spread of COVID. States fought among themselves over who was doing the right things to protect their citizens. One political side blamed the other for not caring enough about mankind or science to follow the protocols put in place. Videos of people violently intimidating or threatening other people to mask up or else circulated on social media. Another political side accused people of living in fear and being sheep, not thinking for themselves but complying with every government demand, no questions asked.

I'd often hear, "JI, your mask," as I struggled to keep one on for extended periods of time because they were uncomfortable. I didn't blame the average working class individual for the polarizing discussions, heightened social tensions, and divisive narratives. They were just following protocol. What I did take note of was the condescending tone of some politicians and celebrity elite. I must admit, I thanked God a couple times for the fact that I lived in Florida, as our leaders in the state seemed to take a more level-headed approach toward tackling COVID than other parts of the nation. Overall, I had no stakes in the game, so I kept my mouth shut. Like most Americans, I just wanted life to get back to normal, and soon.

In mid-March of 2021, the first round of vaccine shots was made available to NBA players and staff. There had been circulating conversations and even swift implementation of vaccine mandates by employers, states, and ultimately the federal government. I didn't like the idea of mandated vaccination, but thanks to our players union, we had a choice. I chose not to take the vaccine.

My decision to not take the shot was informed by a few things. One big ticket reason was I'd already had COVID. So, a part of me was just not afraid of the illness, plus understanding natural immunity after infection put me at ease. I thought it was strange that this topic wasn't being talked about or even addressed, especially as the overwhelming majority of people recovered from COVID at something like a 99.97% rate. In fact, the discussion of natural immunity was actually struck down from social media platforms as disinformation, along with many other ideas that even hinted at forgoing the vaccine. On top of that, adverse side effects and reactions weren't discussed in the public eye by politicians, the vaccine manufacturers, or the CDC. But what really made me uneasy was the subtle pressure applied to conform. There was no discussion. From Twitter to the news to the grocery store, the unspoken message was that if you wanted to do the right thing and if you really cared about other people, you'd take the shot. All this over what was technically a medical procedure. Seemed illogical.

The league made it clear that restrictions placed on the unvaccinated next season would be inconvenient, as a way to encourage its players to vaccinate. What's a couple inconvenient restrictions to the many Americans facing a mandate without a union? I carried on unvaccinated as months went by. The NBA season came and went, but the war around COVID continued.

More importantly in my life, during the 2020-2021 season and summer, I was preparing for a September wedding. In a breathtaking ceremony at the Disney Four Seasons Resort on September 18, 2021, Takita and I tied the knot. What can I say? We are a match made in heaven! Who do you think officiated our union? If it wasn't for Doc, the two of us would never even have been at the altar together.

Rehab, book stuff, and wedding prep kept me busy. I didn't even realize I had picked up a new name in the media: anti-vaxxer.

A TWISTED NARRATIVE

There's so much to unpack around COVID because of how much it's changed our daily lives and because of just how polarizing the topic has become. Unfortunately, the more polarizing a subject is, the less you're able to talk about it in a reasonable way. Here we have a relatively new illness with so many variables and fine details that we are still learning about, yet all we seem to care about is vaccination status. A person's character and moral stance boiled down to whether or not they were vaccinated. You were either a part of the morally superior vaxxed club or you were on the outside, an ignorant anti-vaxxer with zero regard for humanity.

A week after my wedding and a few days before the start of a new basketball season, I was connected through the team to a reporter from the illustrious *Rolling Stone Magazine*. From the start, the reporter assured me that he wanted to have a lighthearted conversation around COVID and the league's vaccination stance. Simple. At first, I was perplexed as to why me, but then I remembered I was unvaccinated.

I agreed to do the article.

I thought our conversation went great. I was prepared, having done quite a bit of research around COVID for weeks on end and had even spoken with some medical professionals about it. I felt I had a solid grasp on my own reasoning for not getting the vaccine and the science behind the relationship between the illness and the vaccine. During the interview, the reporter asked me if the United States government experimentation on African Americans in the past like the Tuskegee Study had anything to do with my vaccine hesitancy, and if not, what was it? I told him no, but that I could see how those studies could cause others to be hesitant. I shared with him that part of my decision was due to the societal bullying that was taking place against the unvaccinated. I didn't like that. I couldn't understand how people had to choose between a shot, which I emphasized didn't necessarily stop infection or transmission of the virus, and their livelihoods. What sort of choice is that? Also, many of those same people already had COVID, so where was the discussion of natural immunity? I told him I was grateful the NBA didn't impose a vaccine mandate on its organization, but I felt for other people who were forced to take it, including those whose religious and medical exemptions were denied. I wanted to stand with those people. I also shared with this reporter that because I had already gotten COVID, was in peak physical shape, didn't have preexisting illnesses or medical conditions, and wasn't even close to the age range of those most negatively affected by the illness, I didn't feel it wise to open myself up to the possibility of having an adverse reaction to a vaccine that wouldn't necessarily stop me from later getting the virus and passing it on. Finally, I threw in the hypocrisy of so many people being against the vaccine when Trump talked about them, only to demand it with the turn of a new president. We ended the call with pleasantries and his appreciation for my stance. Like I said, it was a great conversation.

You can imagine my shock when Sunday night, right before my fifth Media Day with the Magic, the *Rolling Stone* article drops with the following title: "The NBA's Anti-Vaxxers Are Trying to Push Around the League—And It's Working." The content was worse than the headline. The article talked about how I came to my current vaccination status by researching Black history and watching Donald Trump press conferences. Also, that I watched for people to die from the vaccine and put my trust in God.

I was so upset as many people took to social media to slam me for being grossly misinformed and literally crazy. Without hesitation, I shared the news with Doc. He reminded me that truth will always triumph over lies and that I had a perfect opportunity with Media Day being tomorrow to share my views if asked.

I sat in my bathroom contemplating how in the world *Rolling Stone* could pretend to care about helping alleviate the pandemic and willfully misrepresent my position. My press conference the next day went viral, amassing eight million views in a week. I simply shared what I had originally shared with the reporter. Oh, and I confirmed that I did not reach my vaccination decision by reading about Black history and watching Donald Trump press conferences.

There was a similar thread between the underbelly of the COVID vaccine campaign and the BLM organization. The messaging for both goes like this: What's happening is bad. Trust us, we know how to handle/fix it. Our way is the only right way. And the masses of well-meaning people under this chain of command of sorts follow along, no questions asked. There is something deeply wrong with this mentality.

I don't pretend to have all the answers. I can only point you to what I've learned and, importantly, the One who continues to give me the courage and the strength to stand up and not be afraid to tell the world there has to be a better way; there is a better way.

A NEW LIFE FROM A DIFFERENT WORLDVIEW

Writing this last chapter has been the most difficult one for me to write. I'll forever be in the process of learning and growing, and yet to me the ending of a book requires some sense of closure. A nice red bow to wrap up what's been said. Maybe the challenge stems from knowing this is only the beginning of my story. I haven't arrived. I don't even know all the destinations to which God will call me to travel. But through my highs and lows, I have learned valuable truths that have opened the door to me becoming who God created me to be. That's what I'm striving for, on and off the court.

So what does all of this mean? What's the significance of a ball player not kneeling for the national anthem and not being in favor of mandating the COVID-19 vaccine?

Well, like Doc told me, it's the story behind the stand that gives it its backbone.

Writing this book has truly brought to life how eventful my journey has been. I've made progress. I've fallen short. And I've stood strong. Every moment prepared me for the next. I started out as a young boy afraid to believe and afraid to be myself, but I stand today as a man who has found his identity in Christ and is willing to stand for those beliefs.

The biggest revelation in retrospect is that for so long, I didn't understand anything about God or His intentions toward me. I didn't know that He was a friend who loved me for me, with no strings attached. That he only wanted to see me become who He created me to be. I didn't know that, in Him, I'd find everything I was searching for. Love, peace, joy, freedom. I didn't grasp that He cared about my struggles, or greatest of all, that He died to be in a relationship with me. That's the kind of love I needed. The kind of love we all need.

I know that God will never love me any more or any less than He does right now. He loves me if I win the game. He loves me if I lose. He loves us when everything seems to be going our way, and He loves us when we hit the wall. It's out of His love that He desires to help us.

In Jeremiah 31: 3-4 (NKJV), God says, "Yes, I have loved you with an everlasting love; therefore with lovingkindness I have drawn you. Again I will build you, and you shall be rebuilt."

I'm a testament to the truth of that verse. I chose to stand and declare that Jesus is the healing antidote for the hurt and pain that's all around us because He's been just that for me. And like Doc and my local church demonstrated God's love to me, I can demonstrate it to others and champion it as the way forward for the world. Through His love we can bring healing, even if it's just one person at a time.

Learning the truth of who I am—a beloved child of God—gives me the strength to stand for the truth. By God's grace, I'm no longer the same person I was growing up. Seeking validation in points or praise. Trying to perform for love and basing my self-worth on the approval of others. I've come to find my identity in the One who truly gave it to me, and I'm striving along the process of growing my relationship with Him.

I never would have imagined standing in front of millions of people, alone, for what I believed was right. Nor having the courage to preach to a congregation. It's not because I discovered some newfound confidence; it's that through the journey of God working in my life, He's proven Himself to be trustworthy. I'm not special; as you trust in Him, His love, power, and grace extend to all. No matter what your level of confidence is today, God's strength will develop in your weakness.

Once you accept that truth, you will grow to a point where standing alone is better than not standing at all. Then you'll discover, like I did, that you were never alone to begin with. You'll see that taking a leap of faith will inspire others to follow suit and give them the courage to stand up too. Being courageous doesn't mean you're not afraid. The presence of fear is just a sign to depend on something greater than yourself. Courage is found in trusting that God is greater than your fears. Know that you can never stand for Him and He not stand for you.

Everything I've been through along this journey hasn't been easy, but I promise you it's been worth it. Jesus said, "He who finds his life will lose it, and he who loses his life for My sake will find it" (Matthew 10:39 NIV). I've been willing to leave my life behind, and in the process, I've lived a life I never could've imagined. God wants the same for you.

NOTES

[1] Laura Brennan, and Ross Brownson. "South Bronx Greenway Partnership," accessed February 21, 2022, https://www.transtria.com/pdfs/ALbD/Bronx.pdf.

[2] Paul Benger, "William J Seymour – Azusa Street Revival," *Paul Benger* (blog), February 4, 2021, https://paulbenger.net/2021/02/04/william-j-seymour-azusa-street-revival/.

[3] Mike Hopkins, "Providence Extends Offer to 2016 Player from Florida," *pcbb1917* (blog), December 8, 2014, https://pcbb1917.com/2014/12/08/providence-extends-offer-to-2016-wing-player-from-florida/.

[4] Zoological Society of London. "Toads' earthquake exodus." ScienceDaily, accessed February 19, 2022, www.sciencedaily.com/releases/2010/03/100330210949.htm.

[5] Alfy Flores, "Jonathan Isaac shows off star power in win vs. Notre Dame," *FSU News* (Tallahassee, FL), January 19, 2017, https://www.fsunews.com/story/sports/2017/01/19/jonathan-isaac-fsu-makes-presence-felt-vs-notre-dame/96775988/.

[6] Mel was the first Magic representative I met after being drafted. She took me through all of the interviews and helped guide me through the stations of Media Day.

[7] 105 three-point shots from different spots and variations.

[8] One of the trainers

[9] Jason Williams (@55buckets), "I'm scarred for life!!!!" Twitter, August 22, 2020, 7:54 p.m. https://twitter.com/55buckets/status/1297321288076230656?ref_src=twsrc%5Etfw%7Ctwcamp%5Etweetembed%7Ctwterm%5E1297321288076230656%7Ctwgr%5E%7Ctwcon%5Es1_&ref_url=https%3A%2F%2Fclutchpoints.com%2F3-craziest-nba-rookie-hazing-moments-ranked%2F.

[10] 1 Corinthians 3:6-9 (NKJV)

[11] Philip Rossman-Reich (@MagicDaily), " One Media Day observation that surely means nothing, but still stuck with me... Jonathan Isaac seemed so at ease and comfortable with himself. Just a different vibe about him. Don't know what that means, but he isn't a rookie anymore. #Magic." Twitter, September 20, 2019, 5:25 p.m. https://twitter.com/omagicdaily /status/1178782879662432257?s=10.

ACKNOWLEDGEMENTS

TO MY LOVING WIFE, TAKITA, thank you for your unconditional love, belief, and support that strengthen me each and every day. Thank you for always seeing the king in me. Your words and actions of encouragement have pushed me to become a better man, and I'll forever cherish your presence in my life. I love you and cannot wait to see the future God has in store with you by my side.

To Mom, thank you for your heart of love and strength. For always believing in me. I love you and appreciate all that you've done. I wouldn't trade you for the world.

To Pops, thank you for loving me and laying the spiritual foundation in my life that is now being built upon. Carrying on the Isaac name is a privilege and an honor.

To my family, there is no journey without a start. Thank you for your actions of love and words of encouragement. I appreciate you all and thank God for blessing me with the family I have.

To Dr. Durone Hepburn (Doc) and First Lady Phuong Hepburn, words are not enough to express the nobility with which you've taught, loved, and guided me along my journey. This book would not be possible nor would I be the man I am today without your influence. To you I simply say “thank you,” with the upmost respect, and I thank God for you.

To Coach Dennis Gates, may you forever be blessed for doing more than required, every step of the way. Thank you for caring and believing in me when I didn’t believe in myself.

To Ronald Owens, your sacrifice, belief, and love will never be forgotten. Thank you for everything!

To Akii Dean, thank you for your friendship and investment in my life. Seeds that you planted have opened the door to where I am today.

To J.U.M.P. Ministries Global Church, it takes a village to raise a child. Thank you for your prayers, time, and attention. I thank God for giving me such a strong community of loving believers. This is our book.

JONATHAN JUDAH ISAAC is a professional NBA basketball player for the Orlando Magic. Isaac became the sixth overall pick in the 2017 NBA Draft after an impressive season playing for the Florida State Seminoles. While his career stats are impressive, his undeniable heart for God sets him apart. He is a minister at J.U.M.P. Ministries Global Church under Lead Pastor Dr. Durone Hepburn. Jonathan speaks nationally on topics of God's love and faithfulness and Christian unity. Isaac is involved with charity work and continually gives to worthy causes like Project Life Inc., a nonprofit organization that helps to celebrate and protect culture and community globally. Jonathan can also be seen weekly on his show Judah Nation on JGNtv.org and on the JGNtv app.

JUDAH

J.U.M.P MINISTRIES GLOBAL CHURCH

J.U.M.P. Ministries Global Church (J.M.G.C.) is a nondenominational church, birthed in 1992 by founder and overseer Bishop Dr. Durone Hepburn in New Smyrna Beach and is currently located in Orlando, Florida. Dr. Hepburn is a world-renowned speaker, anointed in his gift of prophecy, and has traveled the world to share the Gospel. He is a spiritual father and mentor to many young leaders of today's generation and continues to dedicate his time to teach, impart, and build future world changers and leaders. J.U.M.P. is an acronym for "Joyously Unveiling the Master's Plan," with our foundational scripture found in Romans 8:19: "The creation waits in eager expectation for the children of God to be revealed." The Lord has mandated us to step outside the church's four walls to share His Gospel and demonstrate His love through serving and meeting the needs of His people. Under the leadership of Bishop Dr. Hepburn and his wife, Pastor Phuong Lu-Hepburn, J.U.M.P. Ministries has faithfully served the central Florida community for thirty years through local and global outreach efforts. These efforts have led the ministry to birth Project Life, an outreach ministry that has provided aid and relief to over a hundred thousand children and families worldwide. The ministry has continued to expand throughout the years and now includes J.U.M.P. Global Network (JGNTV), J.M.G.C. Christian Academy, and J.U.M.P. Inn Drop Center, a homeless community resource center.

www.jumpministries.org

PROJECT LIFE INC.

Project Life is a nonprofit organization dedicated to assist and provide relief efforts to local and global communities worldwide. Since 2012, Project Life has provided hurricane relief aid and essentials to over a hundred thousand families, partnered with local and world leaders to provide relief efforts to their local communities. The organization was able to provide COVID-19 relief assistance during the early shutdown period and established a COVID-19 Ready, Set, Feed program, which provided free meals to students and families within the local community five days a week. It concluded with over twenty thousand meals served. Project Life is a collaborative effort of people from many nations, supported by an association aimed to bring awareness of culture, unity, and the message of hope to the world. Through this mission, "The Global Food Festival," was established. This free Christian event was created to bring hope to communities worldwide by providing a positive and uplifting environment. Through the hands of our local church community that is from all nations, we gather together at one event to serve. The event festivities include free food from over ten nations and a gospel concert—and the families receive a distribution of boxes filled with nonperishable food and essentials all from the hands of our local church community. We are proud to share our mission, which has served over a hundred thousand lives throughout central Florida and the Caribbean islands combined. Thousands of supplies, such as clothes, school supplies, baby needs, home supplies, and medical supplies, as well as over twenty vehicles, have been given to low-income households and local community organizations, such as the Women's Centre of Jamaica Foundation and communities that have been affected by any natural disaster. In 2018, in honor of the twenty-five years of dedicated community outreach efforts, the City of Orlando proclaimed July 23 be henceforth celebrated as Project Life Inc. Day.

www.projectlifenow.org

JGN TELEVISION

J.U.M.P Global Network is a family faith-based broadcast network located in Orlando, Florida. The network is a subchannel (ch55.10) affiliate of the SuperChannel WACX-Orlando, the most powerful Christian TV broadcast stations in central Florida since 1988, with over ten million viewers broadcasting through Central Florida, Tampa, and Gainesville. Our network can be seen through Apple TV, Google Play, Roku, Android, and Amazon Firestick. Our program partners are dedicated to inspiring you as well as creatively sharing with you the stories of today's Christian generation. Our nationwide platform broadcasts amazing sermons from dynamic speakers and Christ-centered talk shows that include *Judah Nation*, starring Orlando Magic forward Jonathan Isaac, as well as Christian music videos, dance, modeling, and more. JGN is dedicated to touching the lives of millions worldwide. Visit our website ***www.jgntv.org*** for details and broadcasting opportunities.

A division of The Daily Wire
www.dailywire.com